COACH

THE LIFE AND TIMES
OF US HALL OF FAME COACH

EMIL NASSER

by
Gerald M. Knowles

edited by
Marilyn von Qualen

FRONT COVER

EMIL NASSER IN FAMOUS PICTURE SHOWING A BLOODY KNEE WHICH OCCURRED WHEN HE DEMONSTRATED A TACTIC AND WAS TACKLED BY THE TEAM.

THE BACKGROUND IS A PICTURE TAKEN OF THE BURNING "W" WITH A FULL MOON OFF TO THE RIGHT AT A HOMECOMING GAME IN OCTOBER OF THE 1980's

BACK COVER

The top picture is of the contemporary Standing on the Corner Park noted by the famous song by Jackson Browne and Glenn Frey — "Take It Easy"

Middle picture is a picture of Coach Nasser as a master's degree graduate from Arizona State Teacher's College at Flagstaff, Arizona in 1947

Copyright

Publication date: September 2014
ISBN
First Printing,   September 2014

COACH
The Life and Times
of US Hall of Fame
Coach Emil Nasser

ISBN
1. United States Sports—Nonfiction.

$10.00
ISBN 978-0-692-36571-7
51000>

9 780692 365717

Dedication

The knowledge, experience and passion
that might be found herein is gratefully shared
with my faithful Bulldog teammates—
John, Charley, Freddie, Terry, Arturo,
Billy, Eddie, Jack, and Jimmy— who played for Emil Nasser.

The deepest appreciation must be bestowed on what has become
one of the most inspiring and respected individuals that has
so deeply touched the lives of so many Winslow youngsters.
Emil Nasser

Acknowledgements

Special appreciation is extended to the following for their help in supplying information and identifying graphics used in this book:

Coach Emil Nasser for his hours of interview and sharing of films and photos and for being such an Incomparable Model of Integrity and Enthusiasm

The Archives of Northern Arizona University.

The Kindness and Hospitality of Barbara (Zahnley) Nasser

Producers and Participants in the 1989 "Nasser Roasting"

Members of the EMIL NASSER FOUNDATION

TABLE OF CONTENTS

During his illustrious career Emil Nasser mentored an endless list of individuals including US Marine Corps Captain J.R. Vargas, a Congressional Medal of Honor recipient, and Ron McCarthy, the "Father" of SWAT (Special Weapons And Tactics). Both men are classic examples of the thousands of Winslow youth who cite Coach Emil Nasser as the greatest influence on their lives. Nasser is acclaimed as the most successful and respected football coach in Arizona history, and his receipt of The National High School Coaches Association Hall of Fame award stands out among numerous other distinctions.

Young Emil, born in Napoleonville, La. and reared within the rich, exacting traditions of his country, was immersed along with his parents and five sisters in a Lebanese-American culture exemplifying respect, honesty, compassion and a litany of other expectations aimed at the formation of character. Those values incubated in a small Arizona mining town known to demand loyalty, tolerance and teamwork and a confident "never give up" attitude. These attributes were fused into the young man's persona as a member of the Miami, Arizona Vandals Football Team.

Nasser bypassed scholarships to Arizona State University, the University of Arizona and St. Mary's and became a Lumberjack footballer at Flagstaff, Arizona. He played both ways for entire games, earning a reputation as an awesome tackle. He also boxed, threw the discus, played basketball and was active and popular in clubs and student government. Too, he gained some considerable notoriety for his part in diverse and plentiful legendary escapades.

Nasser survived 60 roundtrip flights over the "Hump" from India to China, supplying the Chinese with resources to battle the Japanese. He excelled in mechanical training, ascending to a Crew Chief position. His unauthorized presence in training films of B-24 fuel systems equipped him to heroically save 15 such bombers from a fire and explosion. Nasser's C-46, "Miss Miami," however, was lost with an on-board crew. Nasser received air medals and presidential citations for his valor and service.

Nasser accepted the position of Winslow coach amid "the Desert Beauty and Mountain Ranges Blue," initiating an unrivaled 35-year career in the history of Arizona football.

Exhaustive drills, long days of precise and repetitious practice along with "doing the right thing all the time," assured success and made Nasser and the Bulldogs one of the most respected football programs in Arizona.

Nasser and his teams boasted career winning records, state and division championships and undefeated seasons in football as well as championships in baseball and track. He garnered All-Star Game coach achievements and dedications with The National High School Coaches Association Hall of Fame award, capping many other Hall Of Fame awards. Too, ever the humanitarian, Nasser was an eager activist on the early forefront of Civil Rights efforts for race and gender.

Over four thousand Winslow students were forever affected in some positive way by Emil Nasser, a legacy confirmed by a myriad of testimonials and superlative characterizations. The stacks of letters sent to this man thanking him for his heartfelt work and productive influence are a treasure to read. He is a man both loved and honored across the State of Arizona, a powerful changer of life, hope and destiny.

Graphics used in this publication come from personal files of Emil Nasser, Gerald Knowles, Northern Arizona University Archives, Winslow High School Annual and the Winslow Daily Mail archives. Special thanks go to these entities.

Preface

Coach Emil Nasser of Winslow, Arizona established an unparalleled record in winning football games and winning the hearts of youth. Two testimonials epitomize the power Nasser had in shaping the character of those who were touched by his character.

"Coach, you were the father I never had, the disciplinarian I so needed, and the example I badly wanted. In my world I am called Mr. Swat, the Godfather of Swat, and sometimes a legend. If I am any of those things it is because you showed me what a successful leader should be." (Ron McCarthy, Los Angeles SWAT leader, Class of 1955).

"You came into our lives at the right time, for early in life, you taught us what leadership, never give up, integrity, compassion, teamwork, morals and loyalty was all about." (US Marine Corps Captain J.R. Vargas, Congressional Medal of Honor recipient, Class of 1955).

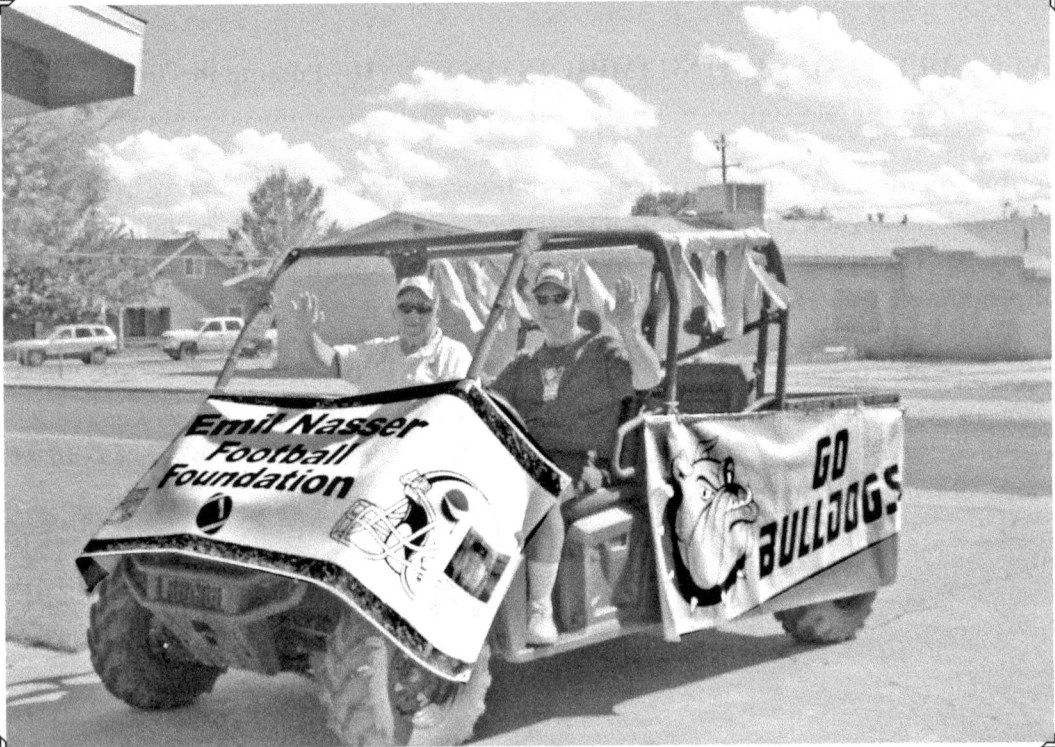

Coach Emil Nasser and Nasser Football Foundation President Joe Benham

BIBLIOGRAPHY

BOOKS
ENCYCLOPEDIA OF THE PEOPLES OF AFRICA AND THE MIDDLE EAST,
Stokes, Jamie. Page 406

LEBANON : A HISTORY, 600-2011, Harris, William W.
New York : Oxford University Press, 2012

MAN AND SOCIETY IN AN AGE OF RECONSTRUCTION, Mannheim, K..
London: Routledge. 1935.

SCHOLAR COMMONS,). "Assessing Druze identity and strategies for preserving Druze heritage in North America," Radwan, Chad K. June 2009.

SYRIA & LEBANON HANDBOOK: THE TRAVEL GUIDE. Footprint Travel Guides. Mannheim, I., pp. 652–563. 2001.

PERIODICALS
AIR FORCE MAGAZINE. October, 2009.

ARIZONA JOURNAL "Nasser Is Inducted Into Flagstaff Hall Of Fame,"
Holbrook, Arizona, Aug 14, 2013.

NAVAJO-HOPI OBSERVER, "Nasser Brought Gridiron Success To Winslow."
Flagstaff, Arizona. October, 21, 2008.

WEB REFERENCES
Arizona Track & Cross Country Coaches Association, *arizonatrack.com*. The Home of Arizona High School / Prep Track and Field Cross Country Results www.arizonatrackcoaches.com, 11 Dec 2010.

THE PRIVATE JOURNALS OF A LANDSCAPE PAINTER, Edward Lear to Lady Waldegrave, Damascus, 27 May 1858, in Edward Lear Diaries:, September 30, 2010, http//www.nonsensilit.org/diries/letterd/letter-t-ladywaldegrave-from Damascus-27-may-1858/.

US Football Coaches'
Hall of Fame—Emil Nasser

ONE

INTRODUCTION—

Will His Like Ever Pass This Way Again?

Coach Emil Nasser of Winslow, Arizona established an unparalleled record in winning football games and in winning the hearts of youth. Two testimonials epitomize the power Nasser had in shaping the character of those touched by his grace and caring.

"Coach, you were the father I never had, the disciplinarian I so needed, and the example I badly wanted. In my world I am called Mr. Swat, the Godfather of Swat, and sometimes a legend. If I am any of those things it is because you showed me what a successful leader should be." (Ron

Capt. Jay R. Vargas
Medal of Honor Recipient

McCarthy, Los Angeles SWAT leader, Class of 1955).

"You came into our lives at the right time,

Ron McCarthy
Father of SWAT

for early in life you taught us what leadership, never giving up, integrity, compassion, teamwork, morals and loyalty were all about." (Jay R. Vargas, Congressional Medal of Honor recipient, Class of 1955).

SOCIAL AND CULTURAL ELITES SHAPE THE CHARACTER OF A NATION'S YOUTH

Coaches are in a unique position to mold values and command character formation of young people, a benign process affirmed by success and achievement in life.

Karl Mannheim, *Man and Society in the Age of Reconstruction*, identifies the "elites" of society as the major forces in maintaining, renewing and enriching the culture. So too does Valfredo Pareto, in *The Machiavellians* identify elites as potent forces in culture. *(Pareto, Wilfred. The Rise and Fall of the Elites: An Application of Theoretical Sociology).* Robert Bly maintains in *Iron John*, a treatise about the original and traditional complex of character regarding what a male should represent, that he is the protector and icon of virtue, leading youth toward emulating cherished ideals that sustain, enrich and extend the quality of the culture.

Particularly significant in American culture is the way in which youth identify with and emulate the lives and character of sport, entertainment, political and governing elites. One famous basketball player claimed, "I'm no role model." Yet thousands of jerseys with his name and number were coveted and worn by young teenage boys. The author's son played one on one at basketball ball camp—a never forgotten and highly influential experience for his emerging persona.

ORIGINS OF CHARACTER

It's a challenge to comprehend what renders certain individuals significant in the lives of those they touch, but as one studies the culture and traditions of Lebanon it is clear that Nasser was greatly influenced by his Lebanese father and mother. The stability among the diverse Lebanese communities hinged upon mutual respect, and the ancient Maronite Catholic Church provided a deep spiritual outlook on life-integrity, service and compassion.

Miami-Globe, Jerome-Clarkdale, Morenci-Clifton and Bisbee-Douglas all produced not only remarkable athletic teams but leaders and outstanding contributors to their state and to the United States—a U.S. Attorney General, an Air

Force General, State Sport Record holders, military heroes, international celebrities and significant leaders in education, industry and government.

Cafes, bars and the drug store hummed with conversations about memorable games and heroes—certain names became iconic for power and skill, while other conversations hypothesized the details and outcome of upcoming games.

Athletic teams were the heart and soul that united those small mining towns of Arizona. The harsh and dangerous lives of the miners were given release by their support and devotion to their teams, especially football. The dual communities were most often intensely bitter rivals, over time recording epic battles on the gridiron—the author being a participant at one time on opposite sides.

Jerome Arizona, in the northern part of the state is the quintessential example of the mining towns' sports teams ethos. Many came to that steep-hilled town to play semipro baseball, and there was a period wherein the high school played only elite teams in football like Phoenix Union and Boys' Town Nebraska.

The Lebanese-American character of Emil Nasser was transformed to another level by his experience as a Miami Vandal football player and by such characters as Coach Nick Ragus, who was both Nasser's Vandal and College football coach.

The triumph of a smaller and lesser talented Vandal team over state Champions and sister city Globe became the lasting model that guided Nasser's coaching career. The quote in the 1938 Miami High School Annual about that game was prophetic with regard to the career of Emil Nasser—"The tie with Globe, uncrowned, undefeated champions of the state, is truly a feather in Miami's cap. The Vandals showed a brand of football that is seldom seen in defeating Globe, the memorial Turkey Day. With one of the smallest teams in the history of Miami High School under his care, Mr. Ragus, the newly appointed head football coach, accomplished wonders. What the boys lacked in size they made up for in sheer courage and persistence."

While not a mining town, Winslow had some of the identical demographics driving the mining towns—" a camaraderie based on the railroading and a deep love

Coach Emil Nasser inducted into the US Football Coaches Hall of Fame

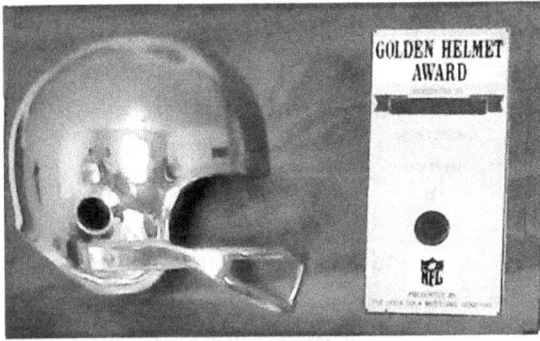

NFL Golden Helmet Award

for its Winslow Bulldog teams.

Rallies began at the old football field initiated by the burning of the "W." The entire student body then joined hands, sang and marched southward 15 blocks down Kinsley Street to the center of town—the future site that inspired Jackson Brown's "Standing On The Corner In Winslow, Arizona." Strains of the school alma mater were aimed at a harvest moon followed by the screaming sounds of pep songs.

Respect and integrity, core elements of Nasser's character, seem rarely acknowledged as guiding principles among some who hold leadership positions of the young and serve as their significant role models. Nasser often remarked, "My Dad taught me to respect and be honest with all people"—concepts too simple and severe for most and all too often almost laughable in some of the school halls of today.

CHARACTERISTICS

Nasser combined intense drill and practice with sophisticated and effective formations, complemented by the development of player skill and fitness.

Nasser was also rumored to initiate audible signal calling at the line of scrimmage as recalled by one Barry Mack.

The "machismo" characteristic in many of today's posturing athletes—sometimes acted out by repeated by violence and abusiveness—seems shallow and weak compared to the honesty, compassion and toughness of the likes of the unsung and unaccredited Nassers of the world.

Heroism and daring were Nasser's mettle during his stint flying the Hump to China — more than 60 missions over terrain wherein failure resulted in a road of no return. That he risked his life without hesitation to save a B-24 and five other B-24 bombers lends a fascinating dimension to his character profile.

A roasting was scheduled soon after Nasser's retirement in the 1980's; 400 friends and a host of former Winslow Bulldogs came from all over the country to honor him. An announcement in local papers and the Arizona Republic about Nasser's 90th birthday drew a crowd of over 200 at the Winslow Elks club. Former players and students come out of their way and make it a commitment to bring their sons, nephews and grandchildren to meet Coach Nasser. It has become an axiom in the life stories of a majority of people that the interface with a certain individual was the most potent and lasting influence in shaping their life and future.

TESTIMONIALS

The running testimonials about the lasting impact that Coach Emil Nasser had on shaping their lives and character are refreshing at a time when there would appear to be a great absence of character among the elites of America.

The long list of testimonials about Emil Nasser's influence on young lives includes individuals across all spectrums of American culture—a Congressional Medal of Honor recipient; a former Federal State Attorney and later Federal Judge; an All American Football player and city councilman of Afro-American linage; a founder and developer of the SWAT tactic of law enforcement; an Arizona Hall of Fame coach.

In every walk of life former player testimonials relate how their work, their whole life's mission was shaped by those few years spent on the red dust and grass along the Little Colorado River in Winslow, Arizona

Congressional Medal of Honor recipient Jay R. Vargas summed up Emil Nasser's contribution: "You came into our lives at the right time of life, you taught us what leadership, never give up, compassion, teamwork, morals, and loyalty were all about."

Looking at the testimonials given by former Bulldogs, the concept of leadership seems to emerge as the power that Nasser had in guiding so many of those young men whose lives he touched; to want to become like, to emulate another person has to be one of the requisites of great leadership. However, the word may be used too lightly at this time in American history, for we find few prominent elites worth emulating or attracting the attention of youth. Yet so many of Nasser's players cite his virtues along with his long-lasting guides to their lives and the attributes they strived to achieve.

Nasser's special talents and charismatic leadership qualities were the ingredients that produced 240 football victories, three state championships, 16 division championships and four undefeated seasons. Such success earned Nasser Football Hall of Fame Awards as U.S. Coach, Arizona Coach and Northern Arizona Coach.

The 1955 Divisional Football Championship Team provided Nasser the highest accolade that a group can give to a mentor: "WHAT YOU DO IN LIFE ECHOES IN ETERNITY-YOU DID IT ALL FOR US, AND WE WILL NEVER FORGET."

Early Beirut and Mt. Lebanon

TWO

FORGING OF CHAR-ACTER—Crucibles That Shaped Greatness

THE LEBANESE CONNECTION

Esteemed Principles of Lebanon

Respect is a word, a concept often lost in a fog of conflict and deceit. Of an early morning in Winslow, Arizona Coach Emil Nasser—Hall of Fame coach many times over— a resounding "respect" broke the silence through the sun's rays pouring across the high desert and Little Colorado River Valley. Yes, it was respect that lay at the core of Nasser's cluster of principles driving him to supreme accomplishments in sports, in World War II, and in his life's service in forging character in every person he touched.

Answers to the question of what it was in Nasser that produced such a remarkable results lie in the rich traditions and culture of his native Lebanon.

The word "Lebanon" comes from the name of the coastal Mountains and is a slight adaptation of a Semitic word for whiteness. The word could also derive from the whiteness of the mountain's limestone cliffs or the snow of Lebanon noted in Jeremiah,18:14—"Does the snow of Lebanon ever vanish from its rocky slopes? Do its cool waters from distant sources ever stop flowing?" — *Edward Lear to Lady Waldegrave*

Lebanon—The Land

"The interior of Lebanon is wonderfully fine—a kind of Orientalized Swiss scenery—innumerable villages dot the plateaus and edge the rocks which are spread on each side of and rise above dark ravines, winding downward to the plains of Tripoli and the blue sea."

—Edward Lear to Lady Waldegrave, Damascus, 27 May 1858, in the Edward Lear Diaries: The Private Journals of a Landscape Painter

Cedars of Lebanon

Lebanon is divided into four distinct physiographic regions: the coastal plain, the Lebanon mountain range, the fertile Beqaa Valley and the Anti-Lebanon

Mountains, (the Western name for the Eastern Lebanon Mountain Range which are a southwest-northeast-trending mountain range that forms the majority of the border between Syria and Lebanon.)

The country's surface area comprises 4,036 square miles of which is 3,950 square miles is land. Lebanon has a coastline and border of 140 miles on the Mediterranean sea to the west, a 233 mile border shared with Syria to the north and east and a 49 mile long border with Israel to the south. Claims to the border with the Israeli-occupied Golan Heights, in an area called Shebaa Farms, is disputed by Lebanon. The coastal mountain range is a historical and geographical core of that country and the main stage for its distinctive social development—an area wherein diverse and distinctive cultural groups live side by side in common respect with each other.

Lebanon's climate is the classic Mediterranean type boasting cool wet winters, hot dry summers and steamy summer humidity on the coast. Annual rainfall varies from 80 inches on the coast to less than twelve inches in the northeast.

The Cedars of Lebanon can rise to a height of 130 feet and supplied wood for the early Phoenician seafaring vessels sailing the known world. Indeed, the Temple of Jerusalem was structured with cedars. The trees were so valuable that they acquired the protection of the Roman Empire. Embedded in the national flag, they symbolize the strength and longevity of the Lebanese people who at this time exist in a malaise of conflict and contention.

Lebanon—The People

Lebanon presents a cross culture of numerous civilizations who have existed there for thousands of years. It was the ancient home of the Phoenicians and over the centuries was conquered and occupied by many— the Assyrians, the Persians, the Greeks, the Romans, the Arabs, the Crusaders, the Ottoman Turks and the French. The impact of all these various cultures created a great diversity of ethnic, linguistic, religious and denominational identities, yet the people share a common culture and Lebanese Arabic is commonly spoken throughout the land. Their food, music, and literature are deep-rooted in the Eastern Mediterranean Region.

Various distinct communities with different religious and cultural backgrounds coexisted within each group—as in the case of the Nasser family being Catholic—and maintained a strong identity while yet finding ways to coexist and get along with other subgroups—hence the power of and the crucial need for mutual respect.

Unique and Distinct Groups

Moronite Catholics

Further analysis would suggest that the origins of character and ethics of Emil Nasser could be found in the communities surrounding Mount Lebanon. His family emerged at a time when there were a myriad number of different sects and cultures coexisting around Mount Lebanon. The dominant group at that time were the Maronite Christians, of whom Nasser's father Fred and mother Salina Francies were members. The Maronites are an ethnic group of people whose members are also unified by a common religious background. They are located in the Levant region (Eastern Mediterranean), considered to be the crossroads of western Asia, the eastern Mediterranean and northeast Africa. They derive their name from the Saint Maron

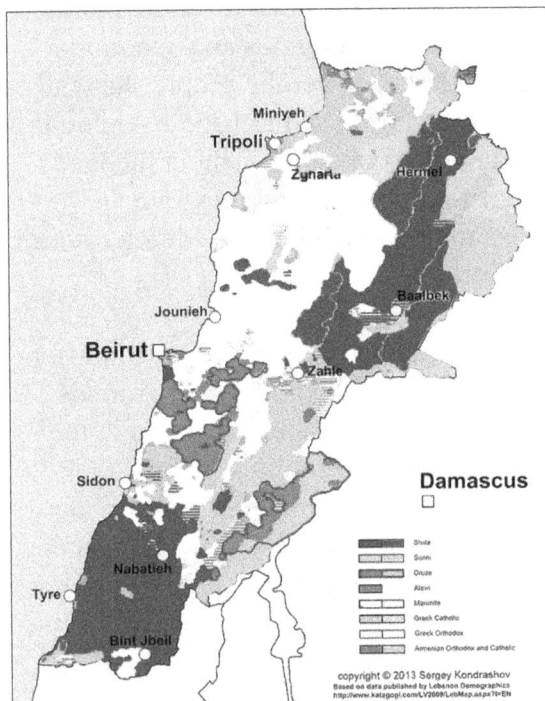

White-Moronite—Dark-Shī'ah Grey-Sunni

of the Syriac Christian group whose followers moved to Mount Lebanon from northern Syria creating the core of the Maronite Church.

According to the Maronite tradition, the Maronite Church, in communion with the Church of Rome, is personally connected to Saint Maron. This tradition has significant value since it represents the followers' thoughts from the middle of the fifth century, the year of 452— the foundation date of the Saint Maron Monastery. The motto for the Moronite Church reads, "No GREATER LOVE, taken from John's Gospel (John.15:13) and expressing the depth of God's gracious love for us in Christ Jesus. It captures the inspiration of Christ's sacrifice on the cross, which calls to each Christian, whatever his or her state in life, and asks us to join with Him in this love and ministry for others." (from the Moronite Church of Brooklyn.) Such a core value is manifested in the character and life of Emil Nasser.

Even after the conquest of the Arab Islamics, the Maronites were able to hold onto their independent status in Mount Lebanon and its coastline. They maintained their religion and language there until the 13th century.

Lebanon was divided into two distinct districts, The Ottoman Mount Lebanon and the Republic of Lebanon, both created as protectorates of European powers with the Maronites as their main ethnic component. Lebanon came under the protection of France, which subsequently had great influence on its language and culture. France established a new country after the Ottoman defeat in World War I, primarily for the Maronites, giving them a disproportionate influence especially after they grew to more than half the population by the 1940s.

Mass emigration to the Americas at the outset of the 20th century and the

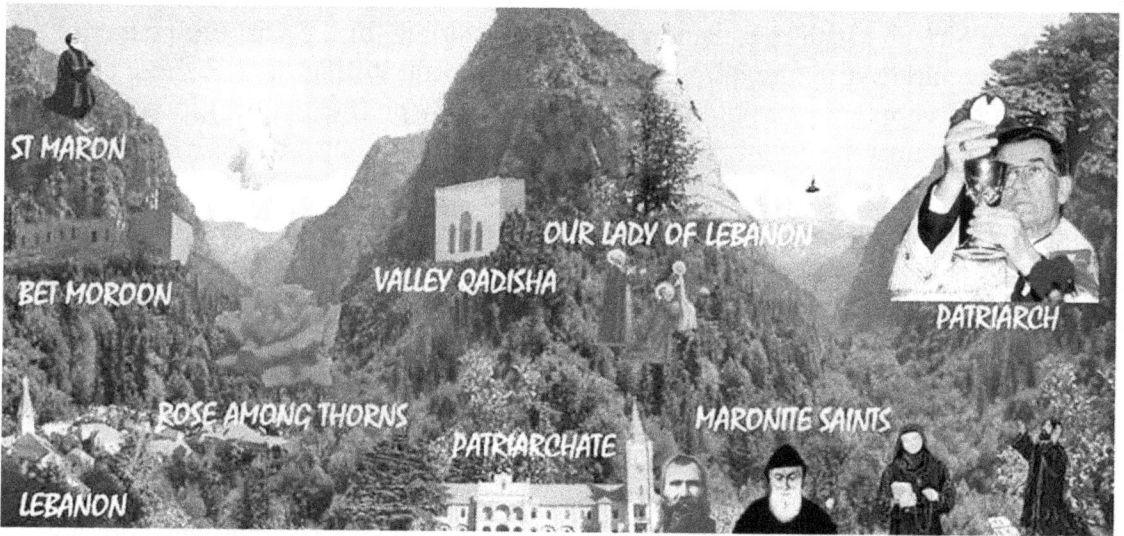

The Maronite Catholic Church - One Fourth of the Lebanese Population

Lebanese Civil War (1975 through 1990), greatly decreased the Maronite numbers in the Levant area. Maronites today form more than one fourth of the total population of Lebanon. With only two exceptions, all Lebanese and Greater Lebanese presidents have been Maronites. The Prime Minister has historically been a Sunni Muslim.

The Druze

The Druze were another key group of people living around Mt. Lebanon; they are a monotheistic community also found in Syria, Israel and Jordan. Druze beliefs combine concepts from Abraham religions, Gnosticism, Neoplatonism, Pythagoreanism and other philosophies. The Druze call themselves "the People of Monotheism" or "the Unitarians." Druze is an offshoot of Ismaelism, a branch of Shī'ah Islam. Druze follow the seven pillars of Ismaelism.

Sunni

Sunni Islam in Lebanon have followers who constitute 27% of Lebanon's population of approximately 4.3 million—around 1,160,000 people. Sunni notables traditionally held power in the Lebanese state and they are still the only sect eligible for the post of Prime Minister. Within the Lebanese context, especially politically, they are seen as an ethno-religious group. Sunnis are concentrated in west Beirut, Tripoli, Sidon and in the countryside of the Akkar.

With the Lebanese civil war ending in 1990 and parliamentary elections being held throughout the 1990's and into 2000, most of the previously warring factions were satisfied with the reforms to the electoral system and took part in the political process. That being resolved, Lebanon's fragile peace was dependent on a sectarian governmental structure where the President is a Maronite Christian, the Prime Minister a Sunni Muslim, and the Speaker of the Chamber of

Deputies a Shīʿah Muslim. Lebanon's re-emergent sectarian structure allows for little cultural, economic, or political discrimination against the Sunni population

Lebanon's Sunni community is among the largest of the ethno-political groups and comprises around one-third of the total population. Sunnis are widely dispersed in Lebanon with the majority of Lebanese Sunnis residing in urban centers (more than two-thirds living in Beirut, Tripoli and Sidon), and rural Sunnis living in the Akkar region, the western Beqaa Valley, and in the Shuf Mountains. They share other Lebanese groups' ethnic Arab background and Arabic language.

Shīʿah

Shīʿah Islam in Lebanon has a history of more than a millennium. According to a CIA study, Shīʿah Muslims constitute 27% of Lebanon's population of approximately 4.3 million—over a million individuals. According to other sources the Lebanese Shīʿah Muslims constitute approximately 40% of the entire population (or 1.6 million out of a total population of 4 million). Most of its adherents live in the northern and western area of the Beqaa Valley, Southern Lebanon and Beirut's southern suburbs. The great majority of Shīʿah Muslims in Lebanon are Twelvers, with an Alawite minority numbering in the tens of thousands in north Lebanon. Few Ismails remain in Lebanon today, though the quasi-Muslim Druze sect, which split from Ismaelism around a millennium ago, has hundreds of thousands of adherents. Shīʿahs are the only

sect eligible for the post of Speaker of Parliament. Within the Lebanese context, especially politically, the group is seen as an ethno-religious group.

FAMILY NAME, ROOTS AND COMING TO

AMERICA

The name "Nasser" means 'victory' or 'triumphant' and may also be defined to mean 'help' or 'endure.' Nasser is Arabic by origin and is a name normally given to boys. It is a very popular name among Arabs and Muslims; one of its variants is Nasser.

Fred A. Nasser

Muslim: from an Arabic personal name based on Nasser 'granter of victory' (*My Heritage Genealogy*)

People with this name tend to be a powerful force for all whose lives they touch. They are capable, charismatic leaders who often undertake significant endeavors with great success. They value truth, justice and discipline, and may be quick-tempered with those who do not. If they fail to develop their potential, they may become impractical and rigid. (*Baby Names*)

"Emile" is a male name of French origin whose meaning is "trying to equal, excel or rival." The name is a variant of Emil, which is Latin, meaning "eager." It is a common male name popularly used as a first name, less so as a second name. During the early period of his life Nasser changed the pronunciation of his name—over the ceaseless objections of his mother—from Emile (Ee-meel') to Emil (Ay'mal)—a more fitting name for a grid-iron warrior.

Emil G. Nasser was born on December 9,

Napoleonville, Louisiana

Selina Francies Nasser

1921 in Napoleonville, Louisiana to Fred A. Nasser and Selina Francies Nasser. Fred Nasser was born in Lebanon in 1871. He grew up there and became a master carpenter and stone builder. His first marriage was to a local girl, producing a family of three or four boys and one or two girls. They lived in a large family home surrounded by acres of orchards and gardens. Early in the 1900's he charged his wife and oldest son, (Wadea, Wade) with the running of the estate while he and other relatives traveled by ship to the U.S. to establish a home and explore opportunities. He planned for his family to join him later. He saved and worked in Louisiana, Mississippi and many mining towns in Arizona—Morenci, Bisbee, Mammoth and Miami. Nasser's younger brother also came to the U.S. Although Fred Nasser was only 56 inches tall and 160 pounds he was very strong, full of energy, very intelligent and spoke five languages. By contrast, Fred Nasser's youngest brother was 6'3" weighed 240 pounds and at a competition at the Hippodrome Arena in New Orleans he earned the title of "The Strongest Man In The World."

Nasser's mother, Selina Francies, was

Nasser, four sisters and Mother, Selina

born in Lebanon in 1896; in 1904, when she was eight years old, her mother, Lulu Francies took her to the United States. She went to school in Louisiana and passed the 8th grade with honors. She married Ellis Faris at age 15 and they had two daughters, Ethel Marie Faris in 1914 and Margaret A. Faris in 1916. Global contention prevailed in 1914 with the start of World War I, those battles lasting until November 11, 1918; concurrently, a world epidemic of flu and pneumonia killed thousands worldwide. Fred Nasser's first wife died in Lebanon; his mother's first husband, Ellis, died in North America. Because of the war Fred Nasser, in Arizona at the time, could not go back to Lebanon. He returned to Louisiana and there he met Nasser's

mother, Selina, through other relatives. She had her two young girls with her and was 22 years younger than Fred. Fred and Francies married and on November 4, 1920 Nasser's sister, Mayme Florence Nasser, was born. In the next year, 1921, on December 9th, Emil was born in Napoleonville, Louisiana. About five months later the Nasser family took the train in New Orleans to Bowie, Arizona and then on to Miami, Arizona, arriving in May 1922. Fred Nasser had a store in "lower" Miami about a mile from "Uptown." His family lived in the back part of the store which had one toilet, one kitchen sink, one wood stove for heat and cooking and wash tubs for baths and clothes. Six kerosene lanterns supplied fuel for cooking and heat.

There were only three regular beds for Fred and Fancies, the two older sisters and Nasser's grandma, LuLu. Mayme and Emil slept in two cribs. A six-foot shelf across the back of the store separated the living area with a five-foot screen for a door. The Nasser family lived in the store for about two years, thereafter relocating across a highway to a house on a hill. Two years later the family moved to Number Three on Hill Street in lower Miami. The house was chosen as it was close to the George Washington grade school. The property boasted a big yard with space for chickens, turkeys and lambs, fruit trees, a garden and grapevines, turkeys and lambs. In 1929 Nasser's parents had a new store built at 511 Live Oak Street, which was Miami's main street. The family business was on

511 Live Oak—Nasser Store

the first floor and on the second floor above there were five bedrooms—a new style house for 1929. $65,000 cash in full was paid for the house and store. (At today's price that would be $650,000.) But after two months in these new lodgings, the Stock Market crashed. The great financial depression began and lasted for the next ten years. It was a difficult time but the Nasser family carried on working

and they all survived. They missed "lower Miami," but Emil and Mayme enjoyed their new schools in town.

Emil's sister Frances Jean "Billie" Nasser came into the world like a Valentine gift on February 15, 1929; Emil's youngest sister, Joan Pauline Nasser, was born on December 20, 1933. The Nasser family was complete—Fred, Selina, five sisters, grandmother LuLu and Emil, the only boy in the bunch. Emil's mother's brother, Uncle Sidney Francies and his two boys, Norman and Dennis, lived or stayed with the Nassers at times in Miami; they moved to Superior and then to Phoenix in the 1930's. Dennis' birthday was on December 8, 1919. Nasser and Dennis celebrated their birthdays together in Miami. Sydney married Nettie Romley in Phoenix; Sidney was Nasser's favorite uncle. Sidney and Nettie had five children—Sidney Jr., Phil, Bobbie and Teeter; they lost one son.

In September 1935 Emil started Miami High School as a 13-year-old ninth-grade freshman. He was the youngest boy in his class. He graduated in May, 1939 when he was 17 years old. Emil was captain of the football team and in 1938 made All State Honorable Mention.

In 1929 and 1930, at ages eight and nine, Nasser worked as a bellhop at the Chief Hotel across the street for $.50 per day plus tips, earning about $.75 to a dollar a day. When he was ten he worked as a helper on produce trucks at a dollar per day at the Farmer's Produce Company. Emil held jobs every summer from 1929 to 1939. The Nasser demand for "toughness and conditioning" may have come from the summer job in which he carried sometimes two sacks of cement unloading a freight card doing heavy construction at the mines for Bechtel Corporation.

At age four Nasser started school, graduating from Miami High in 1939. He was an excellent all-around athlete, and student captain of the football team. He also played basketball, ran track and acted in the Junior-Senior class play.

Emil Nasser's Lebanese and family origins provided an almost perfect makeup for his stellar character and unparalleled achievements. As this chronicle of Coach Nasser's life is written, Lebanon is and has been clouded by a fog of war shrouding the rich traditions of the people who have lived for years around Mt. Lebanon.

MIAMI, ARIZONA—A SMELTER OF CHARACTER

Jerome, Arizona

Arizona Mining Towns

All the mining towns of Arizona have unique beginnings and interesting histories.Miami was founded in 1907 when first developed by the Miami Land and Improvement Company. Miami Land purchased a tract on the upper end of Miami Flats (where downtown present day Miami is located). In 1908 Cleve Van Dyke purchased the tract from Miami Land and also began purchasing adjacent tracts of land. It was not until two days after the first train arrived on the newly constructed railroad, the fourth of October, 1909, did the sale (and renting) of lots begin. At this point, the town was little more than an idea on paper. Only the roughest of streets had been graded, and no utilities of any kind were available. According to the Arizona Silver Belt, 800 people were living in Miami at the beginning of 1910, an impressive number for a town that was only three months old. By the time a federal census taker arrived for the 1910 canvass, there were 1,390 residents in the Miami census precinct.

Miami

Silver mining started in the surrounding areas in the 1870's. Interest in mining gold and silver was far greater than in any other kinds of metal, including copper. It was not until the early 1880's when the price of silver dropped and the price of copper began to rise did the miners begin to take an interest in copper deposits they had previously encountered. Copper ore with content of 5% to over 50% was

MIAMI, ARIZONA

being mined from copper vein and pockets in the area surrounding Globe (seven miles east of Miami), but not in the Miami area. The large deposits in the

Downtown Miami in the '20's

Miami Wash/Pinto Creek area were a type known as porphyry deposits, a term that refers to bodies of ore in which the recoverable mineral (copper) is disseminated throughout the rock mass rather than through concentrated vein or pockets. The porphyry deposit ore typically has only 2% to 3% copper content which was considered unprofitable. Toward the end of the century as the reserves of

higher grade ore (5% or high) dwindled while the demand for copper increased, the copper industry took interest in porphyry deposits. New processes were developed to recover copper from porphyry ore, which made the very large ore deposits in the Miami region profitable to mine. In 1906, the Miami Copper Company began working the claims in the Miami area and the demand for labor in the mines increased. Most of the men traveled to work on foot (no public transportation); few miners could afford to keep their horses. The new mines were located five miles west of Globe. These factors concerning the development of

Original Miami High — 1916

Miami High School Vandals Football Squad ,1938
Co-Captain Nasser #18, 1st Row Center

new large scale copper mines and the need to provide miners with convenient housing, shopping and places of amusement led to the founding of Miami, Arizona.

Nasser and the Miami "Vandals"

Emil Nasser's childhood and teenage life could have been no more significant than

The Miami High Vandals

that of the mining town of Miami, Arizona. Like Jerome and other mining towns in Arizona, the population was a mix of ethnic groups bonded by the miner ethos and a fierce loyalty to their sports teams, particularly that of the local high school football team. Miami's sister town of Globe claimed Irish, Welsh, Polish,

MIAMI, ARIZONA, FRIDAY, DECEMBER 2, 1938

VANDALS FURNISH BIG UPSET IN THANKSGIVING DAY GAME AT GLOBE

Mexican, Chinese and Italian families creating a rich mix of food and festivity. Miami claimed a similar composite of diverse culture—each contributing its unique spirit and ethos to the community's identity. The harsh nature of mining itself produced strong, tough and

Coach Nick Ragus

nual football games became the defining event not only for the rest of the year, but also because the games shaped the character, identity and attitude of the whole town, and in perpetuity. For Jerome it was Clarkdale smelter-town, for Bisbee it was Douglas, for Morenci it was Clifton and for Miami it was archrival Globe just five miles north east.

In September, 1935, Emil started Miami high school as a 13-year-old freshman. He was the youngest boy in his class, graduating May 1939. He was captain of the football team in 1938 and made all-state honorable mention.

agile youth. The hazards of working underground in tricky environments also developed a camaraderie and dedication among the miners which was passed on to their offspring. Yet, when it came to sports, the twin mining-smelter towns of Arizona stood as bitter rivals whose an-

Beginning his football career as a high school freshman, Emil became a Miami Vandal—a prophetic move. However, his father, fearing the consequences of such a rough sport, forbade Emil to participate. So it came to pass that mere tape would

Miami High stuns Globe with a 7 - 7 Deadlock with Nasser Extra Point—Nov. 24, 1938

ries, that Thanksgiving battle featured a game between the Miami "Vandals" and the Globe "Tigers." —".... *The tie with Globe, uncrowned, undefeated champions of the state, is truly a feather in Miami's cap. The Vandals showed a brand of football that is seldom seen, in defeating Globe, that memorable Turkey Day. With one of the smallest teams I the history of Miami High School, Mr. Ragus ... accomplished wonders. What the boys lacked in sized they made up for in sheer courage and persistence.*" (The Miami High School Annual of 1938) Miami had three games in a row and had scored zero points prior to that Globe game

not disguise the broken nose he eventually acquired from ferocious, head-on tackling. After practice one day, he explained to his father that his terribly swollen and bruised proboscis was the result of his running into a door.

That Historic Thanksgiving Victory

The outcome of the annual Thanksgiving Day football game between Miami and Globe inflamed the psyche of the townspeople and moments of the day were relived again and again. Former players for Emil Nasser gingerly circumvented any reference to that game of Thanksgiving 1938 to avoid a two hour replay of every down, of the significant role Nasser played and the riotous mistake made by Globe's main newspaper, the *Arizona Record*. The *Record* which published each Thursday published a holiday special citing a Globe victory. Quite appropriate and most descriptive of Arizona High School Football mascots and rival-

Nasser Graduates from Miami High

For Jerome the fitting mascot for a mining town was the "Muckers," which moniker many claimed with tongue and cheek and which required careful control of the schools cheers. Jerome's competitive teams were so esteemed at one time that they played the major Arizona high

1938 Miami High Annual note of Praise and Prophecy for Nasser by Coach Ragus

schools like Phoenix Union and Boys Town Nebraska. Several other mining towns chose "Bulldogs" as their mascot—alluding to a tough, tenacious, spirit. Winslow Bulldogs during the Nasser reign as its coach connoted terror among many high school teams (as confirmed by a Catholic Priest at Nasser's Roasting who had his parishioners pray for their team prior to Winslow games.) Flagstaff Eagles were the bitter rivals of the Winslow Bulldogs—Winslow being characterized as the blue collar proletariat and railroaders and Flagstaff as populated by college professors, sawmill magnates, businessmen and ski bums. The author's latent schizophrenia could be attributed to having played for both high schools—the days as a Nasser Pickle being the prime time of his life.(note last page).

The Arizona State Teachers College Lumberjacks at Flagstaff

THREE

TRANSFORMATION—

Right of Passage as a Stellar Lumberjack

Nasser Enters Arizona State

Teachers College at Flagstaff

Emil Nasser began his career as a Lumberjack in the mountain town of Flagstaff, Arizona, bypassing scholar-ships to ASTC Tempe, the University of Arizona and St. Mary's. He en-

Flagstaff, Arizona and the "Peaks"

Freshman Emil Nasser

rolled at Arizona State Teachers College (ASTC-Flagstaff) on September 19, 1939 as 17-year-old freshman on a football scholarship. He played both ways for entire games, earning a reputation as an awesome tackle. He also boxed, threw the discus and played basketball. He was active and popular in many clubs and in student government— but he also gained acclaim for his part in what were to become memorable, legendary escapades.

Ariel View of ASTC Campus- Stadium

Nestled as it was in the small Currier & Ives setting of the 1930's, Flagstaff campus life was both delightful and exciting. Not only were the ASTC-Flagstaff students of that time charmed by a faculty devoted to

Lumberjack Field

teaching, but also, students had easy access to an exhilarating outdoors, whether skiing on the San Francisco Peaks or swimming in Oak Creek Canyon— the latter a prominent setting for Hollywood films—and geology classes were embellished by field trips to the Grand Canyon. The white dome of Lowell Observatory, distinguished through Percival Lowell's study of Mars and the discovery of the "Planet" Pluto by Clyde Tombaugh, looked down on the campus.

The traditional Flagstaff 4th of July celebration, the All-Indian PowWow, was at that time internationally recognized for its colorful, inspiring depiction of tribal ceremonies. Too, the area was a hunter's paradise—elk, turkey, deer, quail, geese and duck were abundant and supplemented by some of the best trout fishing in the southwest. The student body mingled with and was affectionately supported by the faculty, establishing a warm and comfortable context for life and learning.

A JAGUAR SWIFT SUMO WRESTLER

Over 50 Octobers had passed since that day in the Lumberjack Football Stadium when a loud 'whack' resounded across the football field and a yellow helmet was seen to pop up into the autumn sky. Out of the mass of bodies stacked at the line of scrimmage appeared a massive hulk with sculpted, Greek-inspired features. Moving like a jaguar-swift Sumo wrestler, the player scooped up his helmet and returned to the Lumberjack defensive huddle. "Fullback Rip Pitts just met Emil Nasser!" Andy Wolf's voice boomed through the crisp October air, reverberating in the stands of Arizona State Teacher's College at Flagstaff.

Lumberjack Nasser—Upper Right

Many attendees that day can still recapture the thrill of their dramatic introduction to one of the most unforgettable people they would ever meet. Emil Nasser was to play a significant part in many lives; he would have a tremendous impact on so many

young men. He would become a football coach standing amongst only a small minority of his American peers in terms of his achievements in an illustrious, 35-year career.

NASSER AS A LUMBERJACK

Nick Ragus, the Miami Vandal's coach and later Nasser's Lumberjack coach, had assembled a cast of characters who truly mirrored the Dirty Dozen of military fame. They were most certainly a group of 'football

THE LUMBERJACK FIGHT SONG OF THE '30'S
When all the Lumberjacks fall in line
They're go'in win a game another time
They're go'in fight, fight for every score
They're goin win their games for evermore
They'er go'in win this game for ASTC!

vandals.' In 1939, in the Thursday edition of the Globe Arizona Record, a state daily newspaper, the headline read, "Globe Defeats Bitter Rival Miami 7 to 0." However—a Yogi Berra déjà vu occurred: "The game was not over until it was over." The game actually ended when Miami tied the game in the closing seconds with Nasser's point after touchdown. Nasser's famous saying, "Winners never quit and quitters never win," entered the annuals of high school football lore and rang often in the ears of his football players.

However, after a few days at the Flagstaff campus Emil found he longed to go back to Miami. As is the case with many college frosh, homesickness had set in and he missed his large, supportive family. Then student body president, Joe Rolle, who is remembered as 'storming' into Nasser's dorm room and firing off a number of epithets, persuaded Emil to 'hang in there.' Rolle, a product of the mining town of Bisbee, later became a long-time friend and honored alumni of ASTC-Flagstaff. Nasser not only stayed for the 1939 school year but

Lumberjack "Bluebooy" is Stuck

was a guard in football, boxed as a light heavyweight and also played basketball, boasting an uncommon athletic range when measured by today's collegiate penchant for specialization. Nasser was given special honors by the ASTC's league, the Border Conference, for his two-way play as a lineman.

In time, Nasser later shared the true origin of his wish to leave campus and go home. It was not homesickness but the fact that he was caught up in the middle of a school prank.

THE LUMBERJACKS

WINNERS NEVER QUIT

A tremendous change occurred with the entry of the Miami Vandals—Nasser, Rentaria, Cisterna and Left halfback Marc Soto. The Homecoming Game of 1946 saw the Jacks as succumbing to the strong New Mexico Aggie team. In fact the Jacks appeared powerless for the first half and went into the locker room behind, 6-2. It would have been 6-0, but Nasser broke through the line and tackled the quarterback in the end zone; the Ag-

gies, putting the ball in play on their goal line, were tackled in the end zone for a safety.

During the second half, Nasser relentlessly piled up the opposition at the line of scrimmage, making his famous helmet-popping hit. Again and again the Jacks stopped the Aggies, mounting a comeback that waxed legendary at ASTC-Flagstaff (now known as NAU – Northern Arizona University). Vince Cisterna, who would later be the first Arizona football player to play in the East-West Shrine Game, caught a pass for a touchdown while totally engulfed by the opposing Aggies. Eventually, Rentaria boomed through the line for another touch-

Nasser in "A" Club for Many sports

down to give the Jacks an upset win of 14-6.

The following Saturday, playing against Colorado State at Pueblo, Nasser blocked a punt, caught the ball in the air and ran into the end zone for a winning touchdown. The author, electrified by the action and by the strains of the cheerleaders—assuredly

Nasser in Basketball

caught football fever that chilly September afternoon.

SUPER CONDITIONING

NO WEIGHT LIFTING ROOMS

In those days, there were no posh weight lifting rooms or training tables, no cadres of trainers to minister to the team. But Nasser had his eye on becoming a professional football player and was devoted to a tough regimen of conditioning. He worked on construction during the summer, taking the dirtiest and toughest jobs available. Daily, he carried 40-pound sacks of cement to the mixing sites. Conditioning and fundamentals were absolutely essential to him, and those same standards were applied to anyone who

later played for him.

At his post-retirement Kiwanis Club roasting in 1984, Nasser was presented a tee-shirt with his likeness captured inside a pickle. The 'Emil Pickle' was the end product of the strength, toughness and agility that characterized Nasser's Winslow Bull-

Nasser was inducted into the Prestigious 13 member " Chain Gang"

dogs, a team that literally struck fear in the hearts of opponents as game days neared. "And please pray for our boys when they play Winslow this Saturday," local Catholic priests often petitioned at Sunday mass.

Bear Meat Beats ASTC-Flagstaff Tempe

The Lumberjacks were facing the last game of the 1946 season with their perennial nemesis, the Arizona State Teachers College at Tempe Bulldogs, which team later became the first in Arizona to win the Rose Bowl under the guise of a new mascot, the Arizona State University Sun Devils. Several weeks prior to the game, Coach Brickey came to think that the perfect diet for toughening the Jacks in prepa-

Nasser in Student Government

ration for that titanic contest would be one of bear meat. Taking Brickey seriously, a teacher named Micke accommodated by killing a 300-pound black bear and presenting it for Lumberjack training table consumption.

The game with ASTC-Flagstaff and the Tempe Bulldogs did turn out to be a bear of a game. Nasser broke through the line, grabbed the Bulldogs All-American halfback and carried him 5 yards behind the line of scrimmage where he dumped him on his back. The Jacks were definitely loaded for bear. Fullback Frank Rentaria made a saving tackle, reaching out with his forearm to smack a sprinting back, flipping him in the air. The Tempe stands nearly flooded the field in rage, claiming foul by Rentaria for using his fist to knock down their star All American. White-hot rage turned into a lasting resentment after the referee nullified as incomplete an end of game pass for a touchdown. The 13-13 tie that ended the game was a moral victory for the Lumberjacks; they'd been the Bulldog's doormats year after year.

The entire Tempe student body met in protest after the game, insisting that if the Jack's Coach Brickey were a gentleman, he would allow the final touchdown. Plans were launched to make a formal protest to the University Board of Regents. The crowd made a solemn pledge that "Tempe would never play Flagstaff again if Frank Rentaria was on the team." He was a dirty player, they claimed, and had slugged and injured several of the Bulldogs. (Dave Rogers, a player on the field and witness to the incident, insists that Rentaria used a flat forearm tackle and never slugged anyone).

Nothing ever came of the protest other than it provided a fitting finale, some rich lore to be shared by the campfire for decades to come. That game was the last time the Bulldogs and the Lumberjacks played. The Bulldogs became the Sun Devils with the Pacific Ten Conference within a vastly expanding university football program that gained national prominence under Dan Devine and Frank Kush. Nasser played every one of the 60 minutes of every Lumberjack game; their impressive schedule included playing the

DINING HALL

Nasser was loved by Mother Hanley and was her assistant

University of New Mexico, the University of Arizona and The University of Texas at El Paso.

CAMPUS ESCAPADES

Mysterious Campus Mischief

Like all college students, Nasser and his football buddies had a fine time involving themselves in innocent mischief in addition to washing dishes for the famous Mother Hanley. Unfortunately, students would sporadically bring dishes with bits of egg or other smudges on them in complaint to Mother Hanley, who in turn would read the riot act to Emil and his friends.

With Mother Selina near Flagstaff

The innocent mischief of men who had braved the traumas of World War II did not in any way suppress the prowess of Nasser and the Lumberjacks. During the war years, material for the Lumberjack football team was thin. Their reputation was weakened and they were typed as underdogs, as nonentities in most Border Conference contests.

Nasser's role as a "Night Rider" is an untrue urban myth which has been repeated many times, especially at his 1984 'Roasting.' It was even suggested that his off-campus exile to the Flagstaff Armory was a result of this behavior as a Night Rider. If the truth be told and even though some of the Night Riders were his football buddies, Nasser was never involved in

Mysteriously, after several months of complaints, the criticisms abruptly stopped. Several students were observed to have become skinheads overnight, one displaying the faint evidence of a half-blue and half-yellow skull. Rumor was that a group called the 'Night Riders,' their heads shrouded in white pillow cases, were shaving the hair off of those who made negative comments about Chow Hall cuisine. Legend also has it that Nasser and several buddies had to live off campus for a period of time before being allowed back into the dorm. It was also alleged that a famous Rose Tree Tavern, located in the middle of downtown Route 66 at that time, was a hangout for some of the Nasser bunch, whose service during the War gave them the extra years to be 'of age.'

With Mother Selina at the Grand Canyon

their antics. Rather, Nasser's dorm violation occurred as retribution for a group breaking into his room and pouring water and dirt all over a set of starched shirts newly arrived from his mother in Miami. Apparently several students had a confrontation with another group of students, and the maligned group sought revenge; unfortunately, they mistakenly chose

Hall of Fame Coach Nasser   27

the wrong room, which happened to be Emil's.

Emil retaliated by going into the perpetrators' dorm room and locking the door from the inside. He turned on the water in the sink, placing a board so the water flow would descend to the floor. He then tied sheets together and went out the second story window.

College officials kicked Nasser off campus to live in the Armory Building. Many believed that he was disciplined for his participation as one of the Night Riders, who, dressed in KKK style hoods, had harassed students who had criticized his kitchen crew for bad dish washing. Although alleged to be one of the "Night Riders," he actually was not involved in that escapade. Ms. Florence Odle did cite him as one of the Riders at his Roasting in 1986. Former President Hughs of NAU also mentioned the time Emil had to move off campus. Actually, Mother Hanley loved Emil and he acted a an assistant cook for one year.

Nasser returned to ASTC at Flagstaff and Lumberjack football in January 1946 for the completion of a Bachelor's Degree in Education and went on to a galactic career. Joining Nasser from the famed Miami Vandals team were three tough mining town stalwarts—Frank Rentaria, Vince Cisterna and Marcelo Soto—whose performance on the field and countenance off the field proved legendary. Nick Ragus, the Miami coach, had since be-

come assistant coach at ASTC-Flagstaff. He brought with him the three Vandals to join Emil in creating one of the most outstanding Lumberjack teams in the school's history.

In that year Nasser earned ten letter awards for football, basketball, boxing and track. In addition he was a student government representative for two years, a recipient of the "Golden Ax" award by the renowned Chain Gang Club, earned both Bachelors and Masters degrees and became an inductee in the NAU Sports Hall of Fame. He was not only a member but the president of the renowned 13-member Chain Gang, a very prestigious, elite group of male students who went through an extremely rigorous initiation ceremony to successfully be admitted as a member. Too, Emil was elected as the Junior Class Representative to the Student Government and was also an active member in the Newman Club for Catholic Students.

Football, 1946: "Despite injuries to

Nasser as Graduate Student

stalwarts throughout the season the Lumberjack football squad went on to chalk up a very impressive mark in the win and loss column. In the season play, the Axers won five games, lost two and tied two. Williams Field Flyers played here on September 14. Wayne See, end, took a pass from George Henry, quarterback, to score as the Lumberjack won 6 to 0." (Arizona Republic, 1946)

On September 21, Coach Frank Brickey had just enough time to whip his boys into shape, and a much improved Lumberjack squad went to New Mexico to meet a highly favored New Mexico Lobo Eleven.

Leading seven to six and with only seconds to go the Lumberjacks attempted to kick from behind their own goal line. This attempt was spoiled when two Lobo tacklers rushed through to block the kick, and recovered the ball for a touchdown. Flagstaff's score came on a pass to end Wayne See. Lobos 12-Jacks 7.

The Lumberjacks won their 2nd game (nonconference) at the expense of a weak New Mexico Teacher's College team by a score of 32 to 0. Coming back for the 2nd half and leading seven to nothing, the Axmen started a rampage and scored 25 points. Touchdowns were scored by Williams, Soto, Casados (co-captain) and Rogers.

Predictions stated that the Fresno State Bulldogs reserves would beat the

Jacks handily. On October 5, the Arizonians traveled to Fresno and battled the Bulldog first stringers to a six-six tie. Cisterna jumped into the air and came down with the touchdown pass.

On October 19, a record homecoming crowd saw a fighting Lumberjack Eleven defeat a strong New Mexico Aggie team 16 to six. Frank Rentaria, a hard hitting back, drove over for one score and Cisterna scored on a pass play.

Colorado State was invaded by air as the Lumberjacks flew over to defeat the Coloradoans 19 to six. Outstanding in this game was Bob Kelly who ran 65 yards to score. Emil Nasser (co-captain) recovered a Colorado blocked punt sprinting 15 yards for a touchdown, and Marcelo Soto, shifty back, raced over for the other score." La Questa, 1946.

Nasser's final year at ASTC Flagstaff culminated in significant achievements. He was such a fierce force as a Lumberjack that he was picked as an all Boarder Conference Tackle. For the first time in history the Lumberjacks tied rival ASTC Tempe. Miami had four of its former Vandals as starters for the Lumberjack—Nasser, left tackle; Cisterna, left end; Marc Soto, left half back; and Rentaria, fullback. Nasser was offered positions as an LA Don pro and as football coach at Winslow High School.

Flying Over the "Hump"

From India to China

FOUR
EXAMPLE OF COURAGE—Surviving Flights Over The "The Hump"

NASSER JOINS THE US AIR FORCE

Nasser entered the United States Army Air Force on July 14, 1942, after completing his third (Junior) year at ASTC Flagstaff. He was inducted in the U.S. Air Force at Fort McArthur, San Pedro, California. He then traveled on a troop train through Flagstaff, Arizona and stopped at Winslow to have lunch at La Posada. The train proceeded on to Sheppard Field Air Force Base, Wichita Falls, Texas. There Nasser attended Basic Training and Airplane Mechanics School until January, 1943. He was then sent to Chanute Field, Illinois for Advanced Airplane and Engine Mechanics, graduating from both schools with top honors. From Chanute, Nasser boarded another troop train to Las Vegas, New Mexico and Camp Luna to await assignment to an actual Air Force base. While there, Nasser lucked out by getting a three-day pass plus a three-day weekend—six whole days!

Nasser bought a ticket to Holbrook, Arizona, hitching a ride south to his hometown at Miami and there spent three days with his family. Catching a ride back to Holbrook he boarded a train to Las Vegas and Camp Luna, arriving a bare 30 min-

A SOLDIER'S FAREWELL. A new recruit kissed his sweetheart one last time before shipping out on a troop train. Along their routes, many trains were met by townsfolk who offered the soldiers food and moral support.

utes before curfew violation!

The next day Nasser and his group boarded a train bound for Detroit, Michigan. A bus retrieved his group and took them to Romulus, Michigan where they were assigned to the Air Transport Command (ATC) 3rd Ferrying Group. They worked on airplanes and did KP duty,

Lieutenant General Chennault's Flying Tigers

guard duty and other minor tasks. Nasser did attend a flight school for B-24 Flight Engineers, and yet was assigned to a

"Trash Crew." After Nasser's graduation from class at Sheppard Field Air Force Base the Air Force "froze" all promotions for three months, preventing him from being promoted to Private First Class as a "one striper"—the first class not to receive the P.F.C. promotion. When an advanced second class was completed one was supposed to be promoted to corpo-

B-24;s

ral—a "two striper." Nasser's class was the last one to graduate from Chanute that did not receive the two stripes. The class that was a week behind their class was promoted because the rating "freeze" was lifted. They kept telling Nasser's group that they would receive their stripes, and to be "patient."

Meanwhile, the group was doing all the

dirty jobs. Lucky for Nasser that he was on the flight line picking up trash behind five brand new B-24's; the planes were from the Ford Willow Run Plant and were getting an acceptance check-up or a preflight inspection. Nasser noticed the B-24 in the middle of the group had all

four engines revving up and 100 octane pouring out of the vent tube on top of a wing, with a large puddle of gas on the ramp! Without thinking Nasser immediately dropped the trash bag and ran to the open bomb bay and climbed up the flight deck expecting to see some young mechanic. Instead, he noted a line chief

Airport—Kunming China

checking out the fuel transfer system.

He looked at the system and fixed the problem, telling the line chief to bring the fire truck to wash the deck and not to "cut" the engines because they might backfire and cause the gasoline on the tarmac to explode.

C-46

A C-46 Cargo Plane Flying the Hump

Nasser remained in the plane until the gas was washed away. When all was clear, Nasser exited the plane to the loud cheers of the G.I.s standing away on the ramp. Nasser then grabbed the trash bag and disappeared in the crowd, hopping on the truck back to his barracks.

The next morning Nasser went into the Line Maintenance Office to ask about his "stripes" and when he would begin work on planes, become a flight engineer or a crew chief.

The office sergeant wouldn't let Nasser see the Commanding Officer. A loud argument ensued and the Commanding Officer came out of his office, asking "What's the problem?" Nasser quickly detailed his story about the promotion

Unloading at Kunming China

"freeze," his waiting time and his training in "picking up trash." The Commanding Officer invited him into his office and told the desk sergeant to locate Nasser's personnel file and bring it to his office; he read the file and told Nasser that he was right to be upset about his status. He

Nasser and cousin Eddie Sawaia

The next six months Nasser flew all over the United States and into Canada ferrying B-24's, B-17's, B-26's and A-20's to modification fields and bomber bases; he then flew back to Romulus (Detroit in Civilian Airlines)—TWA, American and United Air Lines. Nasser's group carried a special priority—military shuttles of B-24's, B-17's, and DC-3's would pick them up.

In August of 1943 Nasser was finally assigned an overseas flight to deliver a B-17 to England. He was all set to go when he was assigned to" Project 8" to start a new Air Force base in India. The base

Himalaya Mts.— "The Hump"

began to look very carefully at Nasser and asked, "Are you the guy who saved the B-24's yesterday?" Nasser said, "Yes, sir." The Commanding Officer rushed over and grabbed Nasser's hand and shook it very hard, exclaiming loudly, "We owe you, and you're a P.F.C. now as a special promotion. Also, I'm putting you on flight pay as a Flight Engineer. Report to Operations Supply and get your parachute, oxygen mask, flight jacket, and other equipment. Also, pick up flight supplies and manuals and attend flight school this afternoon. Don't bother putting your P.F.C. stripes on, because by the first of the month you will be a corporal. You should be ready for your first trip as a flight engineer in three or four days."

According to Nasser, "And that's the way it all happened. I had never flown in an airplane in my lifetime. My first trip in the air was in a B-24, and I was the crew chief and flight engineer."

was established to fly supplies, bombs, gasoline drums, troops, and mules over the Himalayan Mountains to China to supply U.S. and Chinese air bases and armies, "Flying Tigers" and other allies. A large contingent from Romulus Air Force base took the train to the east coast, to Washington, D.C. and on to North Carolina to Camp Johnson to team up with more than 800 other Air Force personnel—pilots, crews, radio men, cooks, clerks, truck drivers and other specialists. Nasser's group was in North Carolina about week for "Overseas Training."

Himalaya Mountains
Between India and China

One day the group was brought into a meeting of 800 other men to listen to the Commanding Officer talk about secret plans and other information. Nasser saw a big fellow about 15 yards in front of him who raised up and began looking around. Nasser thought, "Oh my gosh"—he couldn't believe his eyes! It was his cousin Edward Sawaia from Superior, Arizona. Edward suddenly spotted Nasser who totally forgot about the Commanding Officer's presentation and blurted out, "Eddie!" who yelled out, "Emil!" The two cousins began stepping over men to get to each other, hugging and greeting each other when they suddenly remembered where they were. They looked around and the Commanding Officer had stopped talking and nobody said a word as they stared up at the Commander. He started laughing and said, "They must be long-lost brothers!!"Everyone began screaming and cheering.

The next day they called out 200 men and put them on a train to Camp Patrick Henry, Virginia. The following day the group became an advance party to board ship on the French Liner, SS-Louis Pasteur. The group was on board for two or three days before the rest of "Project -8" group, other air force, infantry and artillery came aboard. The Advance Group was assigned areas and duties in different parts of the ship. Nasser was assigned as the leader of 80 infantry recruits who were fresh out of basic training.

Nasser and the group were located on "E Deck," which was below the water line without portholes. An interesting mixture—a French Ship, British Crew and American personnel. The ship was stripped of all unnecessary equipment

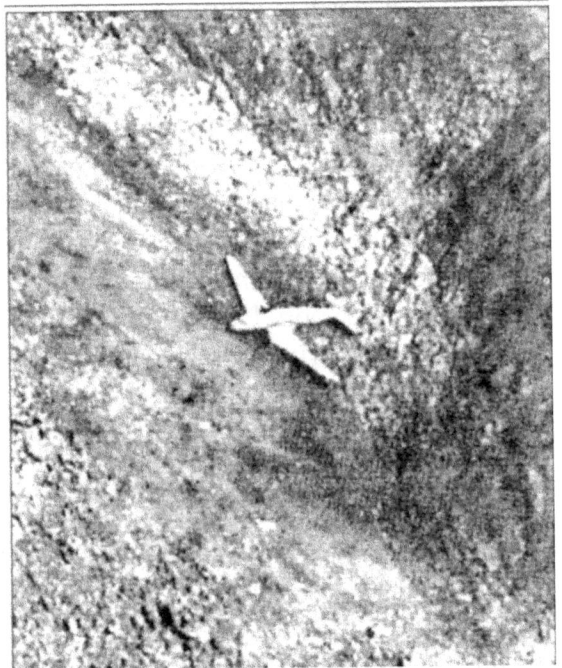

Downed Crews rarely
rescued

and moved very fast at 37 knots or better. There was no escort. Nasser and the group were all alone. They left Newport News, West Virginia and zigzagged for five days to Casablanca, Morocco, North Africa. It was noontime and the group went to Tent City and had only briefly gotten settled and had eaten lunch before they could relax. "Project 8" was alerted.

130 enlisted men and six officers were taken to the rail yards and were assigned

Myitkyina Field, Burma

Burma Road captured by Japanese

to 40' x 8' boxcars, 20 men to each car with two sergeants assigned to each car. The six officers rode in a passenger coach behind the steam engine and the two baggage cars. Nasser was in a middle boxcar. The engine's whistle blasts told them when the train would stop or go, based on long and short 1-2-3-4 blasts. The latrine

had no cover, roof or sides; it was like a steel barrel. They left Casablanca about 17 hundred hours, traveling four nights and three days to Algiers, Algeria. Nasser said they were not told the where, when, who or how—just to be on the train until it got to their destination. Actually, Nasser claimed that the train trip was enjoyable except for long tunnels full of black smoke and the hard drafty floors. Apparently General Eisenhower wanted the U.S. to replace some aircrews that had been shot down over Sicily and Italy. The colonel commanding Nasser's group persuaded him not to break up Project 8. For one solid week they had been living in an open "nose hanger" with piles of

Loading Wounded

Cargo Bay

straw for beds.

Nasser's group was allowed to stick to their original plan. The rest of the group was shuttled by DC-3's (C-47's) to Misamari AAFB 1328 in Assam, India. The group flew in and camped on the Mediterranean shores of Libya, Tunis, Alexandria and Egypt. Nasser visited the Sphinx, the Pyramids and Cairo. He also attended a dance at the Holiday Inn and at the Red Cross in Cairo.

The following day the group flew over Iraq into Abadan, Iran in 100 plus degree heat. Fortunately, the group had a Quonset hut that provided air-cooled quarters. Next they flew to Karachi, India where they spent three or four days waiting for an airplane; they went into the city and fished, rode a camel and ate excellent

Myitkyina under seige

food. From Karachi the group flew to New Deli and Agra where they visited the Taj Mahal Palace. Nasser was amazed at its beauty and joked that their sojourn was like a government paid vacation. The group continued flying, going to Calcutta "Dum Dum" Air Base and finally on to their home base at Misamari, U.S.AABU 1328, where they were stationed for two years.

Cash at Myitkyina Field

During their first month the group got the base organized along with readying their C-47's for the "Hump" flights with 3 man crews (Pilot-Co-Pilot, Radio Man). No flight engineers or crew chiefs. That quickly changed because the pilots wanted the crew chiefs to take care of any problems in China or in flights.

Nasser was making about three to four flights a week over the hump and back in C-47's with gas drums, bombs, troops and supplies. Later the group started getting C-46's to replace the C-47's. The C-46's were bigger, faster and could fly higher, but had more problems which the group finally corrected and modified. The newer C-46's were coming out with fewer issues; everyone was far more satisfied with the C-46's. Nasser never missed a flight (and as crew chief, Nasser

Crew Chief—Flight Engineer Nasser

Nasser soon piled up the trips and combat hours qualifying him for an "Air Medal" and a promotion to Staff Sergeant. He was assigned as a crew chief on a new C-46, #693. He named her after his hometown, "Miss Miami." A girl's picture was painted on the cockpit and after every trip another marker was added to signify a complete mission. "Miss Miami" had eighty missions before being shot down over Burma. Nasser had the flight the day before from the temporary base Alipore near Calcutta, India to where there was heavy ground fighting with the Japanese trying to take over the airport. Miss Miami landed and her cargo was quickly unloaded, and then as Nasser said, "We got the hell out of there and headed back to Alipore." Two small caliber holes were found in the fuselage near the tail. Thirty minutes after they left Mytkyina, Nasser's cousin Eddie Sawaia landed. The radio man on another C-46 was unloading when Japanese planes bombed

had to fill in for any crewmember that was sick or didn't feel like flying his turn).

Crew Chief Nasser and Crew Servicing a B-46

Nasser Chinese Ally Identifier

the runway. Eddie and the flight engineer, Benny Candanda, ran for the slit trench off the runway. A bomb exploded about 30 yards behind then as they dove for the trench. The two of them got hit with shrapnel—Benny in the ribs and Eddie in the butt! Both survived and received the Purple Heart.

The next morning Miss Miami took off from Alipore with Nasser's crewmember Corporal Pennell as Flight Engineer. The plane did not return as scheduled and later that day Nasser got word that she was shot down. The next day Nasser and two of his crew flew with rescue person-

U.S.S. General Callen

nel, piling into three jeeps to within a mile of where Miss Miami had crashed. Nasser and the crew dug through the debris, found remains and dog tags and packed them to the jeeps and then to the plane, flying back to Alipore. It was a long sad day for Nasser and the crew. When they arrived at Missamari, their engineer and maintenance officer Major Peter B. Gash reorganized the base mechanics. Nasser was promoted to Technical Sergeant and Hanger Chief in charge of 100 hour inspections, engine changes and other responsibilities. Nasser was still on flight pay, was scheduled to be promoted to Master Sergeant and had two master sergeants working under him. He also had enough flight combat time for the D.F.C., the "Distinguished Flying Cross" which was scheduled to be awarded to him before he was to be rotated back to the United States.

After the Atomic Bombs were dropped, the war was expected to end sooner than planned. Nasser never heard anymore about his promotion to Master Sergeant and never heard again about a Distinguished Flying Cross. With the war over, Nasser had enough service points to be rotated in the first group— based on the length of time overseas, plus two years

the Red Sea, the Suez Canal, the Mediterranean Sea and the Rock of Gibraltar and across the Atlantic through a terrific storm, arriving on Wednesday, the day before Thanksgiving, at Camp Kilmer, New Jersey. After finally coming in to New York City, the crew spent three days before boarding a troop train to Los Angeles and San Pedro. Nasser received an honorable discharge on November 30,

U.S.S. General Callen

1945. He took a train to Phoenix and a bus to home, arriving in Miami, Arizona on December 1, 1945. Happy Days!!!

combat time, accompanied by citations and awards. Nasser's group was assigned to a troopship, the U.S.S. General Callen in September or October. The ship was unloading troops in New York City and left there to return to Karachi, India to pick up Nasser's group about October 1st, 1945. But when the ship was coming back through the Mediterranean Sea the "Blower" went out and they were stuck in Alexandria and Cairo Egypt for three weeks waiting for repairs and parts. They finally arrived in Karachi about November 1st, 1945.

Nasser's group loaded onto the ship; it took them about 22 days from India to

Bulldogs — Champions of Hard Scrabble, Red Mud and Lime Streaks

FIVE

Building Character—

We Are The Champions—

"The Bulldogs"

Nasser accepted the position of Winslow coach amid "the Desert Beauty and Mountain Ranges Blue," initiating an unrivaled 35-year career in the history of Arizona football.

Exhaustive drills, long days of precise and repetitious practice along with "doing the right thing all the time" assured success and made Nasser and the Bulldogs one of the most respected football programs in Arizona.

THE PRO FOOTBALL OFFER

Nasser graduated from ASTC at Flagstaff

in May of 1947, and his final year at ASTC Flagstaff culminated in significant achievements.

Lumberjack Nasser Decides on Winslow

He was such a fierce force as a Lumber-

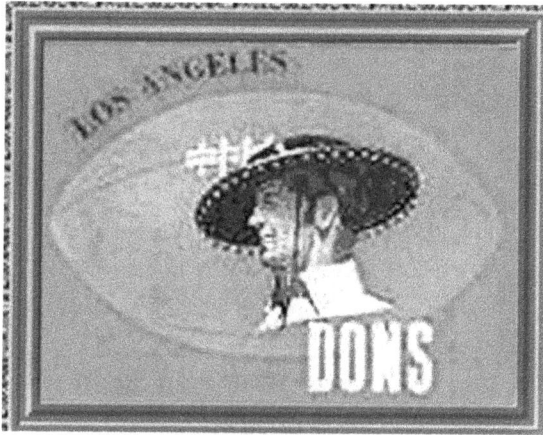

and football, the intense support of the Winslow community and the highly revered status of Arizona's academic program made Winslow the only choice for Nasser. In July, two days before the signing deadline for the Don's job, Nasser was in California practicing with the Dons when Winslow High School's telegram was received offering him the head football coaching position. Ironi-

jack that he was picked as an All Border Conference Tackle. He was offered a position as a Los Angeles Dons of the American Football League—as a professional football player on the one hand, and as a head football coach at Winslow High School on the other. He had a contract in his pocket to play line backer for the Dons, and playing professional football would have realized a lifelong dream. He had also applied for a head football-

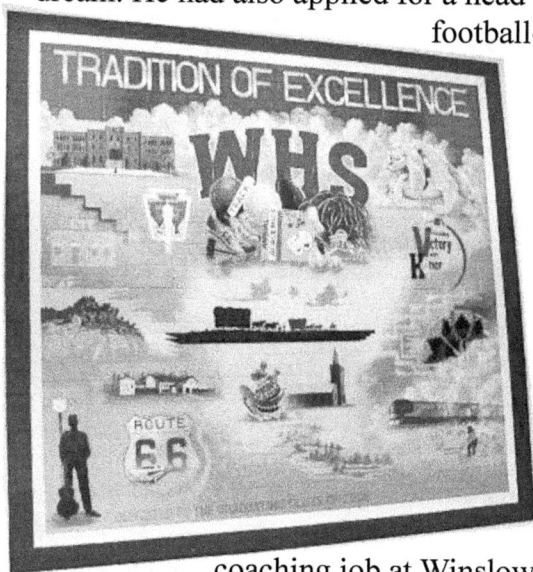

Standin on the Corner
""Well, I'm a standing on a corner in
Winslow, Arizona
and such a fine sight to see
It's a girl, my Lord, in a flatbed Ford
slowin' down to take a look at me"

cally, the spectacular career that was launched in the autumn of 1947 might have never been if that offer had come a day later. He left the Don's team and started coaching in Winslow in August 1947. He coached and taught for 36 years, and semi-retired in 1983.

coaching job at Winslow High School, the only high school in Arizona that captured his interest.

The tradition of sound athletics in track

Like many small communities of the West, Winslow provided a crucible of democracy in the formation of character, commitment and compassion.

Winslow High School was highly es-

"Our Toast To Winslow High
Here 'mid the skies and the
desert's beauty,
And mountain ranges blue,
Touched by the ever gleaming sun-
light,
And desert moonlight too
So we pay homage to you our
High School,
Pledging that we'll be true.
With voice and hand and heart
saluting Here's our toast to you!
With a hep, hep, hep we march
along, Winslow High to you we're
true.
With a hep, hep, hep and a cheer-
ing song, Fighting. working and
rooting for you
You're our pride and honor
Winslow High, You're our inspira-
tion too
For your learning we're yearning,
Hope high is burning,
That's our toast to you!"**

teemed by the University of Arizona; it
produced a U.S. Attorney General, an Air
Force General, a Kennedy Space Center
Director, a Federal Judge, an All-Ameri-

1950 WHS Homecoming Parade

Bell Rang!!!!!!

can Football Player, a U.S. Hall of Fame
Football Coach, world renowned celebrities and Congressional Medal of Honor
Recipient, Jay R. Vargas. Tears often appear in the eyes of Winslow graduates
upon hearing the alma mater:

Jackson Browne and Glenn Frey made
Winslow world famous with the strains of
their well-known song, "Take It Easy" —

Queen Carole Clark

THE BULLDOG'S MYTH IS LAUNCHED

Ultimately, the course of Nasser's career
was neither smooth nor easy for the players or Coach Nasser. As years went by it
was clear that Nasser liked it that way,
and his motto, "When the going gets

FIRST SEASON

A large number of Winslow boys had played sandlot football without pads since the fifth grade, and they could only imagine the comfort of bouncing off the ground and each other clothed in pads. But, they soon found that the novelty of football melted in late August infernos on the red-powdered Winslow practice field. "On your belly, on your back," yelled

tough, the tough get going" could be heard along the football stand sidelines for decades to come.

Freshmen at Winslow High School that August of 1947 were awaiting the onset of football practice with great anticipation, the romance of football having been infused in their very souls from exposure to the Winslow Bulldog sports tradition. Winslow youth kicked off Saturday mornings by reveling in the KOY Phoenix broadcast of the "Adventures of Frank Marriwell"—episodes of a legendary Yale football player who spent his halftimes solving crimes. Autumn days were spent either listening to play-by-play descriptions of Notre Dame or Army games by the famous sportscaster, Bill Stern, or playing tag football on the dusty vacant lots in Winslow. Being a Winslow Bulldog was the dream of many a young boy in that post-war railroad town.

Volume Sixty-Seven   By The Year $2.50

Local Grid Schedule Is Announced

Calls Football Squad

Emil Nasser Calls Meeting Of Football Squad For Monday Morning

With Sixteen letterman from the 1946 high school football squad expected to be on hand, Coach Emil Nasser has called a meeting of all players at the Winslow High School for 9:30 a.m. Monday, August 25.

Nasser arrived in Winslow on Tuesday of this week and began immediately to get everything in readiness to open regular football practice next week. He said he might run the boys through some preliminary practice on Monday as soon as football uniforms had been issued.

A co-captain of the 1946 Lumberjack varsity squad, Nasser also has had football experience during his army career. He was coach and quarterback for an American team organized at Misamari, India, during his overseas tour of duty. At Flagstaff he was varsity tackle and guard, with some experience as fullback.

With the call for candidates for the 1947 squad, Nasser also announced the schedule for the *(Continued On Page Two)*

EMIL NASSER, Winslow High School football coach, who reported this week and has called preliminary practice for the high school football squad for Monday morning. He makes no claims for his squad for the season, but with more than a dozen seniors among returning lettermen he is faced with building for the future from new players, he said.

Competition Is Keen In Rodeo Queen Contest

First Year — First Season

Nasser for over an hour. Such strenuous calisthenics were often followed by a number of laps around the total field perimeter. Helmets had to stay on, and there was no sitting down. Over fifty years later, one could still smell the mud-caked, sweat-infused practice jerseys that hung in the basement of the old Wilson School dressing room.

Ceaseless Drill and Practice

Freshmen in their first season of football began to wonder what they had gotten themselves into. Then again, after practice on sandlot days, there was Kool-Aid to refresh and the delicate touch of the belles of the Gang to sooth bruised arms. Of course the majority of the freshman were members of the Junior Varsity at that time of the season. As game day approached, one aspiring freshman asked when, if ever, "Nasser was going to practice some plays." Three weeks of effort amounted to continuous calisthenics, wind sprints, block and tackle and block and tackle. Players would leave practice and drink a quart of liquid without stopping, sometimes followed by several bottles of pop from the old Blair's Dairy Store across from the high school. One

Nassar Chooses 49 For First String At Winslow High School

Curtis And Lovett Assist In Handling Players; Game Next Week

en pass defense, fundamentals of blocking and tackling, and have done a daily stint of calesthenics. These activities will be continued throughout the season to keep the

First Roster— 1947 Season
(see Appendix A for complete story)

individual (Barry Mack) remembers practicing in a field of red dirt clods which subsequently turned to red powder. When the ball was thrown and landed in the red dust, they could not find it.

Early in the practice sessions players wondered if the torture would ever end. But, as each day passed and muscles were hardened, as skills were perfected and mastery of technique was acquired, they actually began to love every minute of it. A deep admiration for that Jaguar-swift Sumo wrestler coach began to grow. One former Bulldog, who attained his own Arizona Hall of Fame recognition shared that having seen Sumo Wrestlers on TV, he quite imagined that one of them dwelt within their midst—and his name was Emil Nasser.

Such was the case for everyone who went

Front Row: Artis Phillips; Paul Lattin; Don Lowry; "Doc" Watson; Eddie Crozier; Glen Petranovich; Willard Macktima; James Chavez; Cecil Jenkins; Marvin Jennings; Eugene Hernandez; Jerry Knowles; Arthur Rubi; John Bagwell.

Middle Row: Coach Emil Nasser; Dick Werner; Jack Pisel; Clarence Miller; Teeney Davis; Jack Millier; Joe Dominguez; Jack Akin; Danny Patterson; Johnny Castleberry; Jack McCormick; Bill Ames; Bill Burgett; Lucio Ceballos; Noel Archer; Wayne Metzger.

Back Row: Billy Don Stewart; Frank Mosley; Bill Stevenson; David Bealer; Henderson Warnock; George Warnock; Tom Neel; Bruce DeMarse; Harold Walker; George Burney; Jay Fowler; Eulas Oliver; Jim McNelly; Bill Gardner; Bob Dickson; Coach J. Curtis.

First Nasser Squad — 1947

out for football that August of '47. Out of 120 candidates who were suited up to practice, there were only some 60-odd hardened—pickled, if you will—Bulldogs left for the first game of the season on September 1st. With a few simple plays and superb conditioning, the JV players demolished a Holbrook JV that contained half varsity players. The varsity quarterback was so embittered that he left the game and refused to go back.

GAME DAY-VACATION

Nasser's demand for perfection was apparent that first game day. Game day was later seen as a relaxing venture, a picnic compared to practice. Casual observers of coaching personas misunderstood the dif-

Winslow Opens Season With 12 To 6 Victory Over Snowflake Lobos

**First Win— 1947 Season
(see Appendix B for complete story)**

ferences in 'tough' coaching styles, and did not grasp the unique philosophy and techniques of coaches like Nasser. The varsity experienced the same phenomena

Winslow Mail

Volume Sixty-Seven   *By The Year* $2.50   Winslow, Arizona, Friday, October 24, 1947   *Single Copy* 5 Cents   Number 12

WINSLOW HIGH READY FOR CRUCIAL GAME

| Dies Suddenly | Sullivan's Trial Will Go Forward | Navy Day Observed October 27 | Bulldogs And Badgers Of Prescott Meet In Contest Here Saturday |

of unbelievable, sustained stamina and overwhelming bursts of energy in the second halves of games and easily surpassed their opponents' play. In almost every case, the Bulldogs overcame the opponents lead to win in the second half.

EARLY SUCCESSES

The doubts that Nasser had about his decision to turn away from the pros and coach were deep and well-hidden during that first season at Winslow. The 1947 team, Nasser's first, was either tied or behind at half time in every game. Few plays were used, but those they employed had been practiced and honed to perfection. The intense and lengthy drills had literally 'pickled' the players to levels of

Prescott Shows Top Form To Beat Bulldogs 13 To 0

superior toughness, speed and endurance, overwhelming all their opponents except one.

Victory Number 4: Winslow Tramples Jerome, 12 to 6

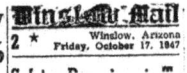

Winslow Mail — Winslow, Arizona, Friday, October 17, 1947

Gradually, in the second half, the opponent's energy and motivation began to deteriorate whilst the Bulldogs increased their momentum, exhibiting an insatiable desire to dominate. Winslow won again and again with second half scores. However, the Homecoming Day arrived when the Bulldogs would face the bane of their existence, the Prescott High School Badgers—rough and tumble cowboys from a place called Chino Valley.

Winslow had not defeated Prescott in over ten years, and their continual trouncing at the hands of that conference powerhouse effectively kept them from any conference or state achievements. Winslow, undefeated in five games, lost to Prescott on October 25, 1947 by a score of 0-13. The defeat devastated Nasser and the team; it had been hard on their bones and it was hard on their morale. "I couldn't handle that first loss, I guess," explained Nasser at an award ceremony fifty years later. The loss itself

46   Coach

was extremely disappointing, but adding insult to injury, it was later discovered that team members might have violated training rules. It was this failure of discipline and commitment that caused Nasser to begin packing to join the Los Angeles Dons.

W.W. Armstrong, the Winslow High School Principal and former coach, inter-

Bulldogs And Eagles Battle To 14 to 14 Draw, Tuesday

See Appendix C and D

cepted Nasser and convinced him of how much had been accomplished and how the kids needed a person like him. He reiterated that there was a bright, promising future for Winslow football with him in charge. Thanks to Armstrong and to Nasser's sheer perseverance, valuable life experiences were ultimately given to an innumerable number of young men.

A former Bulldog player, at mid-season of his freshman year in 1947, had as-

WHS Band — Flagstaff, 11.12.47

sumed a varsity end position vacated by an injured brother of his best and long time friend from Winslow. Even though the former player had moved to Flagstaff the following year, he attended the 1948 Prescott game wherein Winslow won 26 to 7. A 10 second hundred-yard dash man named Louis Lee devastated the Badgers, and Winslow captured the state championship. In fact, Winslow won the annual contest for 19 consecutive years following that game. It was now Winslow who reigned as the most feared and respected

Freshman Letterman Buddies -1947

team of the northern conferences and, later on, of the whole State of Arizona. It got so that no one wanted to play Winslow. Ironically, the 1947 win by Prescott was erased because of Prescott's violation of having ineligible over-age players—making Winslow the un-crowned champions of the Conference. That same former Bulldog also attended a 1948 game in Winslow and was in the locker room when Nasser announced that he had married Barbara Zahnley the night before at the county court house in Holbrook.

Burgett is tackled in the Clarkdale game, Oct. '47 — Winslow 12 - Clarkdale 6

CHEMISTRY OF A COACH

Nasser was a demanding perfectionist about everything that was football: conditioning, fundamentals, play, execution. To the casual observer, even Winslow townsfolk, Nasser's amazing talent was assumed due to his dynamic, high-spirited personality. Years later they came to know that Nasser's greater talent was intellectual. He had created a whole new formation that he called the 'Multiple T'—referred to disparagingly as the 'Nass-T' by opposing coaches. Flankers, men in motion and play changes at the line of scrimmage, a mark of Nasser football, were barely being used by the pros at the time. Nearly all high school defenses deployed a 7 or 8-man line. Nasser innovated with a 5-2 and a 5-3 formation.

Nasser's devotion to excellence caused mothers to complain. Their sons were late for supper. They came home after dark from football practice. Winslow Superin-

First Row: Dan MacLean, Augustus Short, Frank Santistevan, Richard Rubi, Tony Sanchez, Kirl Clark.
Second Row: Coach Nasser, Gordon Campbell, William Hannah, Louis Lee, Cecil Jenkins, Jack Pisel, Jack McCormick, Paul Lattin.
Third Row: Robert Feagins, Herbert Keller, Richard Werner, William Noel, Jim McNelly, Lee Eastman, George Warnock.

First Row: Macario Archibeque, Arthur Rubi, Manuel Ruiz, Dick Bates, Warren Wilson.
Second Row: Glenn Petranovich, Bob Dickson, Jim Coota, Manuel Tamayo, Billy Ames, Danny Watson, John Paul.
Third Row: Boyd Lee, Clarence Miller, Bill Gardner, Eugene Hernandez, Marvin Jennings, Joe Howell, Coach Curtis.

Bulldog Championship Team — 1948 Season

tendent of Schools, one Mr. Booth, once pulled the stadium light switch on a Nasser practice late one evening, but Coach went on practicing by the light of an October harvest moon. On one occa-

Burgett runs left for 9 against Flagstaff
Winslow 6 — Flagstaff 0

sion, an infamous off tackle play innocently termed '#23,' was practiced seventy times on into the Winslow night. Such perfection of execution would have startling results in later years. It would be the '#23' that would win a state championship in the closing seconds of the final game of 1964.

WINSLOW BULLDOGS.

In mid-August tires were spread all over the fields east of the high school, and backs spent hours running miles through tires. If fundamentals or plays were not executed correctly, Nasser would run the ball or block himself in practice to demonstrate technique. Few may be aware that the classic picture of Coach— immaculate in white tee shirt, whistle and football togs—shows a red blotch on his right knee, the result of one of those spontaneous Nasser demonstrations of technique. It was a photo taken just minutes before his famous countenance was captured on film for all to see, *ad eternum*. Players were also charged with running through sage and red sand to distant power lines. One sluggish lineman claimed he went so far one afternoon that he couldn't see Winslow.

"Hoss"

Former players recalling the glory of playing football for Nasser do not men-

Winslow Rolls Over Prescott
First Time Since 1937 Game

Winslow Mail
2 ★ Winslow, Arizona
Friday, October 29, 1948

See Appendix F

tion being chosen all-conference, nor do they mention any particular achievement or award. Rather, they are obsessed with the most prized of all accolades. The most cherished desire held by a Bulldog was earning the ultimate honor, and that was to be called 'Hoss'—short for 'horse.' Being identified in this way was tantamount to being dubbed a Knight of the Round Table. 'Hoss' was a Nasser term of respect and indicated that the individual concerned embodied all that he, Nasser, expected of himself and his players. Few were given the honor. Those that earned it never fail to mention it as the core of their Winslow Bulldog experience. Lonnie Foster, former Bulldog and recipient of the Arizona Coaches Hall of Fame award, complained that Emil never called him "Hoss" until the night he congratulated him at the award banquet. Foster said he always resented never being

called "Hoss" and almost fainted when Nasser finally gave him the tag the night of the award ceremony in Phoenix.

Nasser was also a master psychologist and in that sense reminds one of Knute Rockne's ability to inspire football players. On one occasion, a particularly imposing team from southern Arizona came to Winslow to play a crucial game on a freezing November Saturday. The opposing team left the bus and sat on the benches, buffeted by the cold winds that claim the Little Colorado River Valley in November. Nasser kept his players in a warm dressing room, but when it came time to field his team, they appeared without warm-up and with Nasser in his shirt sleeves, totally demoralizing their opponents from the warm southern desert. It's never been confirmed, but stories abound about Nasser turning the

WHS Annual-'50

"A" SQUAD FOOTBALL

FRONT ROW: Joe Brady, Richard Rubi, Bill Willis, Jim Cooata, Arnold Wolfe, Tony Sanchez, Terry Newman, John Burton, Albert Greer, William Hannah, John Paul, John Brady.

SECOND ROW: Pete Van, Bert Rhoton, Lyle Jenkins, Kirk Clark, Frank DeGraff, Bill Noel, Herbert Keller, Dick Bates, Frank Santistevan, Fred Rubi, Buddy Campbell.

THIRD ROW: Emil Nasser, Jim MacLean, Hubert Snell, Cleve Barber, Carl Clark, Bobby Hendry, Charles Reynolds, Lee Eastman, Bill Church, Boyd Lee, George Warnock.

1949 Bulldog Football Champions

The Burning "W" And Pep Rally — Soul And Heart Of Winslow High

sprinklers on the opposition's pre-game band performance. Nasser flatly denies sending his Bulldogs through the Flagstaff Pep Squad at half time one November afternoon.

Trick plays were carried out in the 1940' and 50's. One such play involved the bulldog quarterback (Cecil Jenkins) complaining of not getting his first and ten. He asked the center to hand him the ball and said he was going to take his first and ten. He began marching into the St. John's High School backfield, all of whom parted to let him forge on by, and on he went until the Winslow players begin giggling and St. John's got wind of the trick and yelled "grab him." Jenkins almost marched across the goal line to a touchdown.

Another trick play which actually worked several times involved the center putting the ball behind one leg, faking a center to a back who faked reception of the ball and raced right. In the meantime the guard next to the center—actually a back placed strategically next to him without violating positioning—wrapped his arms around the center's leg and the ball to a count of three seconds and then stood up and raced to the left. On one occasion the two actually raced untouched over the goal line.

Nasser's mastery and grasp of the game of football and his ability to 'talk' to the subject was phenomenal. Sportswriters and radio announcers would attend post game sessions that could have been assessed as abject lessons about the sport. Winslow assistant coaches would sit in awe at Nasser's analytical, lengthy discussions and dissection of games. Nasser recalls and recounts in great detail every aspect of games played decades ago.

Hall of Fame Coach Nasser 51

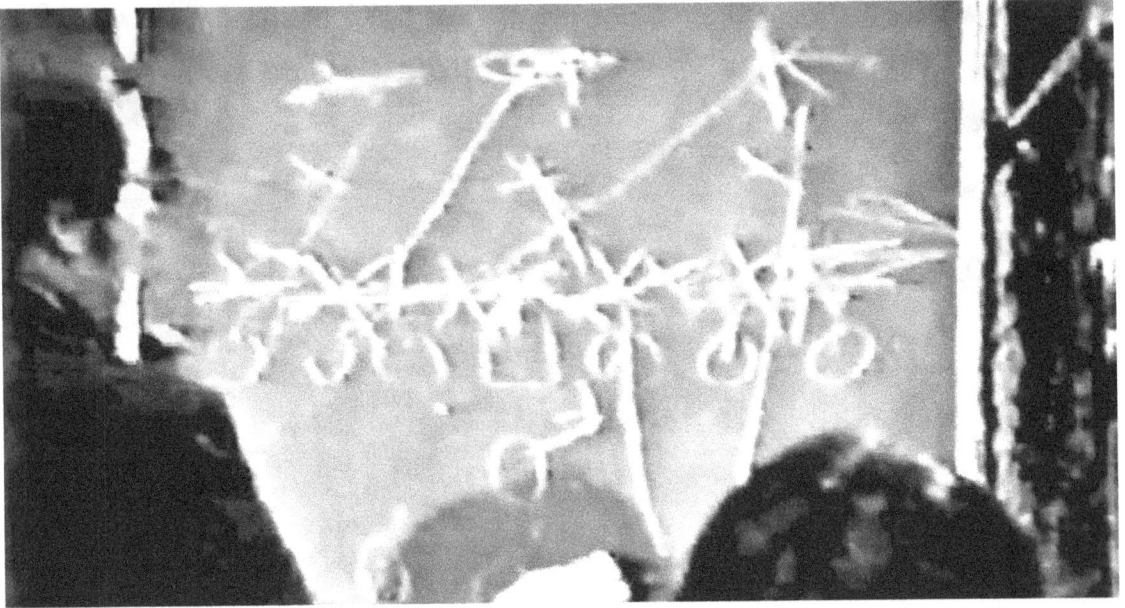

The Famous Nasser "NAS-T"

However, one evening, having wearied of an overlong session on a local radio program, one of the assistant coaches outside the glass door to the office caused a 'moon' to appear when their was no moon in the sky. It's been said that was the only time in his thirty-five year career that anybody ever saw Emil Nasser speechless.

Kinsley Avenue and Route 66 — Right of Passage Altar for Bulldogs

Nasser inducted into the US Football Coaches Hall of Frame

SIX

Epical and Matchless Excellence—Conquest and Fame

Nasser and his teams boasted career win-

Integration — Winslow Pool

Red, Martian-like Desert

ning records, state and division championships and undefeated seasons in football as well as championships in baseball and track. Nasser garnered All-Star Game coach achievements and dedications with The National High School Coaches Association Hall of Fame award, capping many other Hall Of Fame awards. Too, ever the humanitarian, Nasser was an

1955 CLASS "A" NORTH CHAMPS

WHS Annual-'56

See Appendices H through L

eager activist on the early forefront of Civil Rights efforts for race and gender.

HISTORICALLY THE WINNINGNESS COACH

Nasser's 35-year career at the same high school—Winslow—set a record in the state of Arizona and inspired a juicy

Lee scores his first touchdown of the season

WINSLOW 48   FLAG 0
1955 Champions

repertoire of football lore and legend. Nasser would prepare the field for Satur-

day's game on Friday afternoon, the process beginning with the city's steam-roller packing the fine, red Moencopi mudstone dust into a cement-hard sur-

Arizona Coaches Association Hall of Fame
See Appendix M

face. This activity was followed by sprinkling the field with water, which practice tended to produce small, scattered puddles of red mud into which opponents would land, much to their dismay. The Bulldogs however were used to this red, Martian-like desert of a field where they were veritably pickled in the August heat.

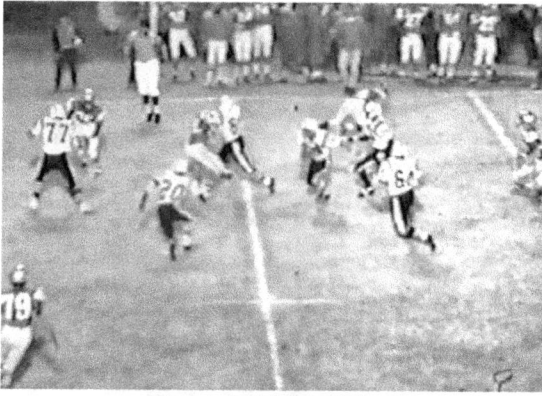
Downfield Blocking

One former Bulldog remarked that it was like playing football in a Wal-Mart parking lot.

The toughness of the Winslow teams was illustrated over and over again by the reactions of their opponents. Having been duly ground into the red dirt for three quarters, an opposing fullback was observed jumping back out of a huddle, telling the quarterback, "Hell no, I'm not going to take the ball. You run it this time."

His Winslow teams won 243 games, lost 90 games, tied nine games; won three state championships in 1948,1949 and 1964; 16 division championships and 13 games as the All-Star Coach for a total of 300 games.

Arizona Track Coaches Hall of Fame

He was the head baseball coach for six years during which he won five division championships—1949 to 1954. He was head track coach for 11 years, winning 11 division championships—1948,1962 to 1969. Nasser was the Winslow High School athletic director from 1972 to 1977. He held the position of Arizona In-

ARIZONA COACHES ASSOCIATION

FOOTBALL

COACH OF THE YEAR

EMIL NASSER

1964

Arizona Coach of the Year—1964

Nasser "Wall of Fame"
See Appendix #

terscholastic Association Region 1 Commissioner for three years, from 1963 to 1966.

Nasser never structured a weak season.

The 1964 Bulldog State Football Champions—See Appendix O

During a short, seven-game slate season, Albuquerque High School—with an enrollment of 4,000—called Winslow High,

Madeo 6 Points for Bulldogs
See Appendices O to W

a very small school——to ask the Bulldogs to play on an open date. Nasser said, "Hell, yeah, we'll play them. The bigger the school, the better." Although Winslow lost by a small margin, they were the only team that year to score on Albuquerque. "The bigger and better the program, the more I wanted to play those teams,"

Bulldogs Playing For State Title Tonight

Winslow's Bulldogs are facing Flowing Wells on the Caballeros' home field in Tucson tonight for the state Class A championship.

See Appendix S

Nasser declared.

HALL OF FAME HONORS

Nasser excelled in getting players to reach in and tap their capabilities, to access spiritual resources they never knew they had. He once threatened to dress a defense in women's clothes if they didn't muster up some aggression. He gestured to them and yelled, "Come on, girls,"

Volume Eighty-Four   Winslow, Arizona, Monday, November 30, 1964   (Associated Press Leased Wire)   Number 94

Bulldogs Win Third State Crown

See Appendix T

when signaling the return to the field after half time. "Practice makes perfection" epitomized Nasser's driving passion and his pride in the Winslow Bulldogs.

Nasser's recognition encompassed not only local, but institutional, state and national citations. He was named Arizona

Championship Team Honored At Annual Quarterback Club Banquet

"If a player gives everything he has—100 per cent—that is all anyone can ask of him," said head coach Frank Kush of the Arizona State University Sun Devils in addressing the Winslow Football Banquet last evening at the Elks Auditorium.

Coach Kush was featured speaker at the annual gathering where Florentino "Tine" Lopez and Mike Madeo were chosen co-captains of the 1964 Bulldog State Football Champions, and where coaches, players and boosters were recognized as the season closed.

More than 400 parents, players, coaches, school personnel and students crowded the auditorium to hail the champions and the other football players of Winslow High School.

Thirty-four varsity players and two varsity managers were honored as the climax to the evening's plaudits. Certificates had already been awarded to

in life, coach Kush said:
"Don't curse!
"Don't gripe!
"Don't alibi!
"Don't get discouraged!"

Dr. Harry Simmons was master of ceremonies for the annual Quaterback Banquet, jointly sponsored by the Elks and Babbitts.

After the invocation by Fr. Richard Milligan, James Nottingham, Loyal Knight, welcomed the football players and their supporters. Appreciation was expressed by Curtis, after which Dr. Simmons introduced guests, including sponsors, coaches, and committee members.

Head Coach Emil Nasser reviewed the season, then introduced Ellis McIntosh who presented certificates to the freshman team, assisted by Dean Stotts.

Nasser then introduced coach Jim Freeman who presented the junior varsity with certificates, assisted by Alvin Fritz.

The varsity squad then was introduced and received their letters. Nottingham presented Elks awards to Everett Patterson, art teacher, coach Carl Weatherton in absentia, and to coach Nasser.

W. M. Wright, assistant high school principal, introduced the guest speaker.

Following the address, the Pep Squad lead in the singing of the WHS Alma Mater.

Other awards, from the teams, went to Trainer Herman McArthur, and coaches Weatherton and Nasser.

Varsity lettermen named were these:

Bill Baca, Curtis Bardsley, Fred Basgal, Pat Beckwith, Bill Bollin, Bill Cherry, Ricky Donnelly, Jerry Easley, Willie Fish, Steve Garner, Art Griffith, Warren Hardy, Bill Heath, John Hysong, Tom Kanuho, Mike Lopez, Tine Lopez, Mike Madeo, John Martinez, Charles Mayberry, Steve McArthur, Rusty Meikle, Mike

CAPTAINS — Tine Lopez, left, and Mike Madeo, right, were named co-captains of the 1964 Bulldog state football champs. They are shown with Frank Kush, ASU Coach and featured speaker at the Quarterback Banquet. (Bergman Photo)

See Appendix W

High School football Coach of the Year in 1964. He was inducted into the State of Arizona Football Hall of Fame in 1971

Assistant Coach Carl Weatherton, Head Coach Emil Nasser and Trainer Herman McArthur

and the Arizona Coaches Association Football Hall Of Fame in 1984 at a ceremony at the Pointe in Phoenix, Arizona. Nasser was appointed as a charter member in the first-class of an Arizona University Sports Hall of Fame in 1981 for his prowess as a Lumberjack at Northern Arizona University (the Arizona State Teachers College.). Nasser's fame beyond the Arizona State border arrived when he was cited as National High School Region 8 Football Coach of the Year In 1982. He was also recognized for excellence in track and field coaching, being inducted into the Arizona Track Coaches Association Hall of Fame in 2004. Ultimately, Emil received the highest honor awarded a high school football coach—induction into the United States Football Coaches Hall of Fame.

The Honors

Coach Nasser's record and the honors he accumulated represent one of the most remarkable careers in high school football—not only in Arizona, but also on the national scene. Nasser's record of 234 wins, 90 losses and nine ties place him only second in the history of Arizona high school coaches. The record was ac-

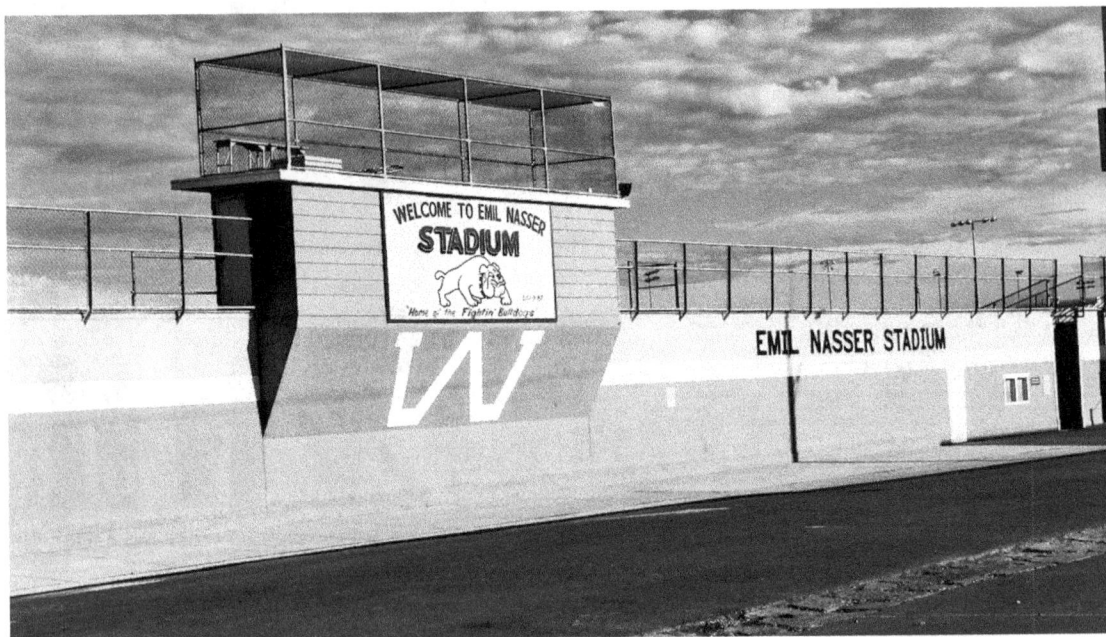

Dedication of "EMIL NASSER" Stadium—September 29, 1989

complished even when only nine—sometimes only seven—games were played. The Winslow Bulldogs won 16 Confer-

EMIL NASSER
SEPTEMBER 29, 1989

IN RECOGNITION OF YOUR MANY
YEARS OF DEDICATION TO THE
WINSLOW SCHOOL SYSTEM, THE
GOVERNING BOARD OF WINSLOW PUBLIC
SCHOOLS DEDICATES THIS FOOTBALL
FACILITY IN YOUR HONOR.

THE W.H.S. FOOTBALL COMPLEX
IS NOW NAMED

EMIL NASSER STADIUM

THANKS FOR MAKING WINSLOW YOUR HOME.

ence titles and three state championships. Nasser, also a track and baseball coach, won nine conference and two state track titles, and five conference championships in baseball. Nasser's 35-year tenure at Winslow High stands as a record for a coach at a single high school.

Formal recognition of Nasser's remarkable feats began when he was chosen Arizona Coach of the Year in 1984. Twice he was invited to coach the Arizona All-Star North team. As early as 1971, he was inducted into the Arizona Coaches Hall of Fame 11 years prior to his retirement. In 1981, he was honored by the Northern Arizona University Sports Hall of Fame; in 1997, NAU cited him as one of five Centennial Alumni. In 1984, the State of Arizona further honored him by inducting him into the Arizona Coaches Association Hall of Fame. But the capstone of recognition of Nasser's stature as a person and a coach came in 1996 when he was chosen as one of only 50 coaches to be inducted into the U.S. High School Football Coaches Hall of Fame at a ceremony in Connecticut.

Nasser family at Stadium Dedication

Nasser claims he had been conning everyone in the sense that he was doing exactly what he enjoyed and wanted to do in a community that was incomparable in its support and loyalty to him and his pro-

gram. He also attributes much of his success to his supportive wife, Barbara, and his wonderful children Danny and Ellen.

Rhetoric, accolades and honors often fall short of what Nasser truly meant to the lives he touched. Joe Dominquez, a halfback on his first Bulldog team of 1947, spoke of qualities acquired from knowing Nasser—toughness, understanding, judiciousness and compassionate concern for players on and off the field as well as inspiration and respect all around in huddle. Nasser was a remarkable person—a player's player, and a coach's coach. Dominquez ended his note by stating that we "love you, and always will." Joe said, "I wish the very best for you, 'Jocko,'" knowing that now, he could get away with saying that.

One fellow, who played first-string end for Nasser that season of '47, moved to Flagstaff the next year. By 1950, he was allowed, albeit reluctantly, to play foot-

ball. After a Flagstaff November victory in Winslow, the last game of the season, he faced a somber, hostile group of former Winslow teammates and members of the Tucker Flat Gang who felt that he, Rusty, had turned traitor. After the team dinner at the Monte Vista Hotel in Flagstaff, Rusty announced to his dance date that he would not be accompanying her. He had a bus ticket, he said, and he was going back to Winslow to hang out with his Tucker Flat chums, one of whom had given him a fierce charley horse.

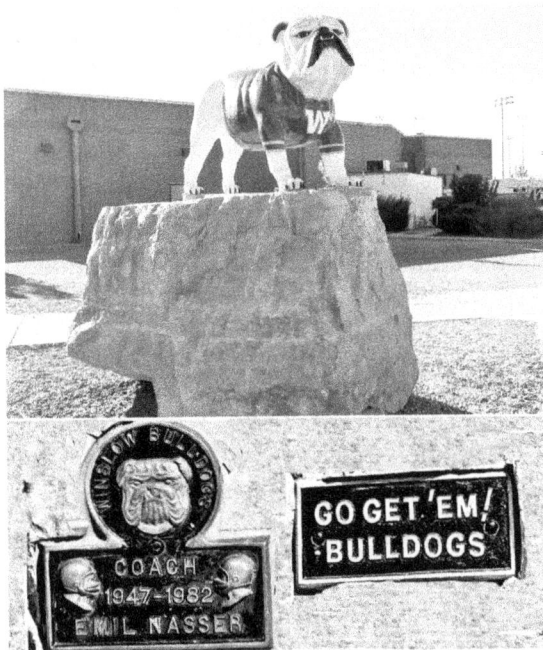

Bulldog "Rock"

Even before the arrival of Emil Nasser,

Winslow High School maintained a tradition of burning the 'W' before football games. Once the 'W' was ablaze, the entire student body would join hands and sing the Winslow Alma Mater. A chain of students would form and they'd chant their way down the street, finally ending

THE FLAGSTAFF HALL OF FAME BANQUET —INDUCTION OF COACH EMIL NASSER

Former Governor Rose Mofford, Arizona's first female governor and secretary of state, was a childhood friend of Nasser when she lived in Globe and he in nearby Miami. She wrote an interesting item for the banquet. It read as follows:"While I did not grow up with Emil Nasser–after all, Globe and Miami were great rivals–his exploits in high school were well known in our Gila County towns. I will never forget the 1938 Thanksgiving Day football game when Emil led his fellow Vandals to a tie with our mighty Tigers (and came very close to beating us). He continued this same desire to win as a player at Arizona State College in Flagstaff and as a coach of the Winslow Bulldogs. Bulldog supremacy during the '60s is still legendary."

up at the center of Route 66 in downtown Winslow. There the cheerleaders brought the crowd to a fever pitch—"Winslow Born and Winslow Bred, and When I Die There'll Be a Bulldog Dead!" One cannot help but feel that the spirit of the Nasser Bulldogs will always be present at the

burning "W"—through all seasons, and far into the future.

If there is any one thing that epitomized the high stature accorded Nasser, it was the simple title used to address him. The night of his roasting, President Hughes of Northern Arizona University, Arizona State Senator Tony Gabaldon, the Mayor of Winslow, a U.S. Hall of Fame high school football coach and former players holding prominent public, athletic and business positions all addressed him as 'Coach.' In doing so their voices resonated love, respect and not a little awe. Even in such remote spots as Puerto Peñasco, Mexico, "Hi Coach" can be heard ringing out across the waves of the Sea of Cortez.

Nasser was honored by more than 40 awards, citations and plaques including recognition from Governor Bruce Babbitt, Governor Rose Mumford (See Appendix #)and Northern Arizona University Presidents Lawrence Walkup and Eugene Hughes. He also received honors and recognition from the City of Winslow, Winslow Public Schools and civic groups including the Rotary Club. The most significant recognitions however came from the Arizona Interscholastic Association, the National Football Foundation, and the College Football Hall Of Fame's "Outstanding Coaches Award." And of course there was his induction into the Miami High School sports Hall of Fame.

Nasser was able to desegregate the Winslow swimming pool in a very effective, but non-confrontational way. Up until 1948 the swimming pool was only open to non-Caucasians the last day before it was drained, i.e., after it had been used steadily for five days.

Emil gained permission from the school superintendent booth to use the pool for classes during May—and of course all students in an integrated fashion swam in the pool during their P.E. sessions under authority of Winslow High School and the supervision of coach Nasser. Since the ice had been broken and the community had been sensitized to an integrated pool, the next step of opening regular summer usage of the pool to Latinos, African Americans and Native Americans was a rather easy step. Local parents and prominent individuals once challenged Nasser as to why there were so many "Indians" playing on the team, especially in the backfield. Nasser's answer was a question—how bad do you want to win? The intense identification and loyalty of the Winslow community and their need to having winning Bulldog teams trumped any anti-racial and anti-ethnic influence on the performance of the Bulldogs. Some of the 1960's and 70's push for civil rights brought issues to the community and inevitably seeped into team relations. Many remember Nasser stating that as a Lebanese American, he was the only minority in the football program. Nasser put policy into practice by refusing to use any venue or service practicing segregation or discrimination, including motels, hotels, restaurants and any other and all discriminatory venues.

One of his former players who was a member of the Navajo tribe (Ted Wilcox) commented on how Nasser would tell stories on the bus for several hours—from Winslow far into Oak Creek Canyon. Wilcox wondered why all the stories were about camels and bandits and not about cowboys and Indians. The team members coined the name Camel Jockey, or Jocko, and were terrorized for fear Nasser might find out. On one occasion a parent (who shall not be named) came into Emil's office with a gun insisting that Emil promise to place his son on the starting team. Emil told him that he was committing a felony, that he would not bend to his request, grabbed his gun and lectured him on how foolishly he was behaving. Ironically, he was one of the Bulldogs who later thanked Nasser for "touching his life," saying that he would never forget him.

Nasser was a towering supporter of both high school and college sports. He became a certified and very active official and referee in basketball, baseball, track, and football. He initiated the planting of grass on all athletic fields, both city and high schools which removed the hard-scrabble gridiron the Bulldogs had played on for so long, and he helped build a new high school stadium for football and track. The complex was named Emil Nasser Stadium, "home of the fighting Bulldogs," in 1989. As athletic director, Nasser started many new girls sports—basketball and track among others. He taught swimming lessons, life-saving and scuba diving—offered free to more than 2500 people in the United States and Mexico. Nasser acted as life-guard and swimming director for thirty six years.

Parallel to coaching activities Nasser was celebrated as a football and basketball referee in college and university games. One of his standouts later became an all-American who played for northern Arizona at Flagstaff, (NAU). During a game at Flagstaff, NAU playing the Texas team of McMurry, the former Bulldog and now Lumberjack wore thick glasses. On that horrible snowy day, Nasser would stop the game to clean Hannah's glasses. Finally the McMurry coach called time and asked Nasser, "why you stopping to clean that 'boy's' glasses?" Nasser told him that "was his boy and if he asked any more questions, his team (McMurry) would be off the field." Nasser was deeply respected by players, parents and the community, and valued as well all across Arizona by other coaches and university programs.

A complete summary of Nasser's record, Hall of Fame awards and honors can be found in Appendix Y.

"Your words echo into eternity
You did it all for us — we will never forget you"

1955 Team

"You will stand watch, O human star,
burning without a flicker, perfect flame,
bright and resourceful spirit,
each of your rays a great idea—
O torch which passes from hand to hand
from age to age world without end."

(Cepek)

SEVEN
THE DEEP AND LAST-
ING IMPACTS ON
YOUTH—Passing the
Torch, Age to Age

INTEGRITY AND CARE

Unlike some prominent coaches of the time, Nasser never abused players but only demanded that they reach deep down inside to tap the spirit and talent that he knew was there. When a Coconino High player was seriously injured, Nasser drove to Phoenix and went over the heads of nurses and officials to com-fort and encourage the injured player. Nasser absolutely forbade any 'dirty' tactics, maintaining that teams could win on the basis of ability without resorting to unfair play. Players who played dirty were sidelined, sometime for entire games.

When one of his first season players was in bed with a serious kidney disease, Coach Nasser personally came to visit him and, on one occasion, produced a bedroom award letter ceremony. Mel Hannah relates that when his 1960 Lumberjack team stopped at the Winslow Airport on their way to play for the National Small College Championship in Florida, Nasser presented him with an envelope full of money. Hannah doesn't know where the money came from, but believes that much of it was from Nasser's checking account.

On another occasion during that championship Lumberjack season, Nasser, also the Dean of college football referees, was working a Lumberjack game amidst mud and snow. After each play he would take Mel Hannah's thick glasses and wipe the mud off them. Finally, the opposing coach confronted Nasser, who in turn said, "That's my boy"—adding other unmentionable comments that squelched the coach's complaints for the rest of the game.

WINNERS IN LIFE

One sportswriter stated that those who played and won for Nasser went on 'to win at life.' Those winners included a director of the Kennedy Space Center, county sheriffs, ranchers, legislators, a U.S. Federal Attorney for Arizona, a federal judge, a hall of fame coach and other successful coaches, university and professional football players, lawyers, doctors and a quarterback and Jay Vargas, who was awarded the Congressional Medal of Honor for heroism in Vietnam. Winslow High School was highly regarded, and not just for football —universities in Arizona sought out Winslow High grads and welcomed them.

Among those graduates were an Air Force General and an Attorney General of the United States. On numerous occasions, coaches and others bringing a young person to see Nasser observed that just meeting the man, simply being in his physical presence, had an inspirational effect. One such individual, not even knowing who Emil Nasser was, commented that he felt something very special occur in a brief encounter. One might well speculate that in our rapidly changing, often cynical world that a strong sense of caring, optimism, and commitment may be all that is needed to turn someone onto the right path.

Players at times coined nicknames for Coach and lived in terror that he would somehow overhear them and find out. At his 1984 post-retirement roasting, former players dared using the nicknames out of affection knowing they had nothing to lose. Because of Nasser's Lebanese-American heritage, they'd referred to him as a 'Camel Jockey,' or 'Jocko' for short. The risk of being discovered caused one former player to smudge out this reference to the Coach in his scrapbook. One naive freshman addressed Nasser on the streets of Winslow as 'Jocko.' Nasser held him upside down by his ankles until he apologized.

THE ONLY MINORITY MEMBER

During the social upheavals of the late 60's and early 70's, the national preoccupation with heritage even seeped into the small railroad town of Winslow. Personal conflict along racial and ethnic lines often threatened disharmony within the Bulldog teams. To the credit of Nasser's character building, his instilling of 'team spirit' and his focus on the superseding value of the importance of every player's role in winning, personal differences were suppressed in pursuit of successful team work. Ethnic and racial disparities were not overlooked, but Nasser's players learned that people should be judged and accepted not by the color of their skin, but by the quality of their character.

Nasser emphasized and demanded sportsmanlike conduct. He insisted that "you do not hate are opponents, but you need to go out there and hit them hard, harder, and harder!!" Jay Vargas echoed such a mantra in a tribute to Nasser and he demonstrated it in winning the Congressional Medal of Honor.

' One outstanding Navajo student explained how Nasser would tell Camel Jockey and tribesmen stories on the bus, beginning at Toonerville outside of Flagstaff and continuing all the way to Indian Gardens in Oak Creek Canyon, some 60-odd miles away.

THE ROSTER

Mel Hannah, who went on to play for the Lumberjacks in a national small college championship game, maintains that in his first season at Eastern Arizona Junior College, the coach excused him from blocking and tackling practice. The coach maintained that Mel, a Winslow Bulldog, had mastered those fundamentals already.

A close friend of the author and a member of the infamous Tucker Flat Gang once took Nasser at his word and, expressing that deeply ingrained self-confidence, called his own play and threw a pass on fourth down on his own fifteen yard line. Fortunately for the preoccupied Nasser and the health of his heart, the pass was completed for a first down.

One frightfully powerful Chicano player, compounding his belief that every play was supposed to be a touchdown, had a penchant for running toward and over defensive backs. On a pleasant autumn afternoon, with a clear shot for a touchdown at the 20-yard line, 'Turo' instead ran right for and over the top of the defensive back, scoring a touchdown. Still, Nasser benched him for a quarter for his lack of discipline.

The few players who earned the famous Nasser handle 'Hoss' also maintained that they had to forebear 'Nasser in their face'—Nasser so close up that they could see between the gap in his two front teeth. "Wah, wah, wah," was Nasser's quick and simple way of reminding players of the need for humility and the mending of their ways.

IMPACT

Youth into Men

Nasser was a master at developing youth into men. He felt it was important to give kids a chance to play football, kids who would otherwise be on the streets being chased by the cops. In actual fact, Nasser's teams were made up of individuals who probably should not have been playing football, but Nasser would always find a spot for fellows who were eager to learn and willing to discipline themselves toward excellence.

Nasser held to strict rules about training—no smoking, no alcohol and no staying out after curfew. He also demanded good behavior off the field—courtesy to teachers, no fighting, respect for all students, male and female—as well as broad participation in all aspects of school life. These principles were faithfully upheld even if they threatened the loss of a game, even the loss of a championship. Nasser once refused to play Flagstaff on a muddy field and the opposing coach

Lee Wasdon

claimed the game forfeited, which could cost Winslow a probable conference championship. Upon examination, it was shown that officials from both high schools had agreed to cancel the game, plus neither team showed up in uniforms ready to play. Thus Winslow legitimately claimed the championship that year of 1948.After that season, Winslow and Flagstaff, staunch rivals, played two games, the first in early September when the Flag field was still green and dry. Players could not suit up on game day unless each teacher signed off on an eligibility slip. A good number of Native Americans who later secured Ph.D.'s, Judgeships or other outstanding posts maintain that they would not even have

graduated if it wouldn't have been for stringent academic standards and the persistence of such great instructors such as Vera Ore, a high school history teacher.

Nasser insisted that football players not isolate themselves as self-styled jocks but that they play in different sports and participate in choir, band, drama and other school activities. Nasser's opening remark to the 1964 team was that they were probably the worst team he would ever coach in Winslow. Even key players felt that they were mediocre in size and ability and frankly, they didn't expect much success.

Before the first game that season of 1964, Nasser announced to the team that they were undefeated and un-scored upon. The team beat Holbrook and prevailed in all their games that season, garnering the Class A Championship. The winning touchdown was scored in the last few seconds of the game by Mike O'Haco, (dubbed the slowest half back in Bulldog history) in a play called #23—the same play O'Haco had practiced 70 times earlier in the season, in the light of the October harvest moon.

TESTIMONIALS BY FORMER PLAYERS

Testimonials by former players over Nasser's 35-year career would fill volumes. A sample of what such testimonials would say comes from letters written by the 1955 division champion team. One of the highest tributes is inscribed on the bottom of a plaque given to Nasser in 2005 from the entire team—the fiftieth reunion; it read, "What you do in life echoes in eternity. You did it for us and we will never forget you."

"He is man we learned to admire and respect, even if there were times we thought maybe he was a little too tough or his expectations were a little too big. We learned much about football, more importantly we learned about ourselves and life—that experience, molded by his character and personality,

Ron McCarthy

continues to influence us, whether we are aware of it or not." (Brian Story)

"This message is long overdue, but with the passage of time, I have an ever-clearer perspective of your influence in my life. As you may recall, I was living in Winslow for a brief time and then left for Tucson, Flagstaff, and Nogales. From Nogales, on

my own, I returned to Winslow. The reason I returned was very simple; it is where I felt the happiest and safest. Returning to Winslow brought me back to you and your influence and guidance.

I was living on my own and wasn't eligible to play sports for one full year. I had to work to eat and staying in school with no visible reward (playing sports) was hard to reconcile in this kid's mind. You were my salvation.

Coach, you were the father I never had, the disciplinarian I so needed, and the example I badly wanted. Because of your impact on me, I stayed in school and got to play one year of Winslow Bulldog Football—one of the happiest years of my life. You were my leader, my example, and my hero. You still are

I have gone on to be successful and happy. In my world now I am called Mister SWAT, the Godfather of SWAT, and even sometimes a legend. If I am any of those things, it is because you showed me what a successful leader should be.

Barry Mack

Thank you Coach, You will always be in my heart."

We were playing Tolleson and for some reason the 2nd string was in. I had just about got the play I wanted to run set up. Lee Wasdon came into the huddle and says, Mack, Coach wants you to run a 'diagonal' Me, I said what the "F" is a diagonal. Nobody in the huddle knew. I said 'Lee you want to score?' and of course he grinned and said sure, so we ran a quick 31 28. Bobby faked great and Lee was five yards outside the end and corner back. Needless to say he scored. Coming off the field Nasser grinned at me, slapped my helmet and said good call. At the ban-

quet he introduced me as Barry Mack, the only player he ever had that was smarter than the coach. And he was not demeaning in any way. (Ron McCarthy #90)

What he taught me was: Everybody has something to contribute. No matter how big or smart you are some one person can always teach you something. He always had faith

Jay Vargas

in us as a team and as individuals. God bless you and thank you for all of it." (Barry Mack)

"You came into our lives at the right time, for early in life, you taught us what leadership, never give up, integrity, compassion,

Charlie Rose

teamwork, morals, and loyalty were all about." (Jay R. Vargas Congressional Medal of Honor Recipient).

"I would like coach Nasser to know how much I appreciate all he taught me about hard work and working together to achieve a common goal. He had an interesting sense of humor. He always wanted us to put our socks and shoes on first after showering in case there was a fire and we had to run outside. Didn't want us to burn our feet, but I guess a barbecued "spanker" was OK. Coach taught that you can always do a little more than you thought you could. He taught me that things of value did not always come easily. He taught me to believe in myself and the synergy of a team that pulls together. The dusty hot days during the summer—2-a-day practices are still a vivid memory. I remember the pep rallies; the burning of the @W" — words seem inadequate to fully express my appreciation to Coach Nasser. You are the greatest. Thanks for the memories and the lessons learned." (Charlie Rose)

Arden McCrae

"You have been one of the greatest influences of my life. I wish my son had met you and played for you." (Arden McRae)

"Your influence on my life and all the people and players that attended this

Bob Belton

gathering will never be forgotten. Thank you for touching my life. The very best to you always." (Rightly Carnutte).

"Thanks coach for being a great messenger in life skills. I learned them well.

Joe McAdams

You taught toughness and means of success, and that stayed with me all my

KEY ROLES OF IMPACT

Winslow High School Athletic Director and Physical Education Department Head.

A certified referee for football and basketball, a baseball umpire, track starter, judge, and meet director for 35 years

Arizona Interscholastic Association Commissioner for Region I for four years.

Director of the Winslow City Pool for 35 years.

Taught more than 15,000 adults and children swimming, life saving, scuba, and water skiing lessons.

life." (Winstel Belton.)

"I never played much but I used the lessons of teamwork every day of my life. Thanks for giving me sound lessons in my life." (Joe McAdams.)

Epilogue

Long after retirement, Nasser revealed to a sportswriter and long time follower of the 'Big Maroon Machine' (Paul Switzer, Arizona Daily Sun, September 27, 1997) that "Football was only a game to be used for the higher purpose of teaching about life." This tenet was confirmed over and over again by the accomplishments of those who had played under Coach

Mel Hannah—1955 Tean
Small College All-American

Nasser.

"Never the Lowered Banner, Never the Last Endeavor" (Sir Ernest Shackleton)

One can not help comparing the spirit and determination of Nasser to that of Sir Ernest Shackleton of Antarctic fame.

Shackleton overcame both impossible conditions and insurmountable obstacles that would have defeated the faint of

heart and brought his crew out of the ice-locked Antarctic across eight hundred miles of sea to safety—"Never the Lowered Banner, Never the Last Endeavor."

Nasser was once recalled as the head coach to deal with and heal hazing problems that arose and damaged the football program. Nasser assisted the administra-

tion, assistant director, coaches, parents and faculty in doing a great job to eliminate the problem.

One of Nasser's greatest satisfactions was helping to end the discrimination directed toward minority athletes and students at cafés, hotels and swimming pools in Arizona. Nasser began working with these issues as soon as he started coaching in 1947. His dedication inspired other coaches to assist in what proved to be successful efforts.

Nasser's wife Barbara and his family were very supportive and loving during his long career. They all enjoy traveling, vacations, water sports, hunting, fishing and exploring the hidden bays and canyons of Lake Powell by boat. They spent many glorious days at their beach cabin in Puerto Peñasco, Mexico (Rocky

Emil

Danny

Ellen

Barbara

Point). Emil coached a high school football team in Rocky Point for 2 years—1997 and 1999. Emil and Barbara traveled all 48 states and also drove to Alaska, across Canada and deep into Mexico. They took trips to Air Force reunions, family reunions and weddings. They also flew to Taiwan, Hong Kong, China, Bangkok, Burma, Singapore and Hawaii for 28 days in 1985. And he circled the globe twice.

From 2000 through 2005 Nasser volun-

teered as an associated coach for the neighboring town of Joseph City. He coached Joseph City football for five

years, taking their team to state and earning two state titles and participation in five state playoffs

Emil Nasser is blessed with his wife, Barbara of 68 years and counting, his son Dan Nasser of Phoenix, his daughter Ellen of Flagstaff and sisters Frances of Phoenix, Arizona and Joan of New Orleans, Louisiana.

He is preceded in death by his parents, Fred A. and Selina F. Nasser, daughter, Cheri Ann Nasser and sisters Ethel and Margaret Faris, Mayme Jonovich, Uncle Sid Francies, Denis and Norman Francies and grandmother LuLu Francies.

He enjoys the company of his six grandchildren—Michael Emil Nasser, James Daniel Nasser, Cole Joseph Nasser, Aprile Fousel Diaz, Tara Danielle Dickens, Staci Michelle Dickens, Frank Dickens and Diane Palmer. Great grandson, Paolo Emil Nasser.

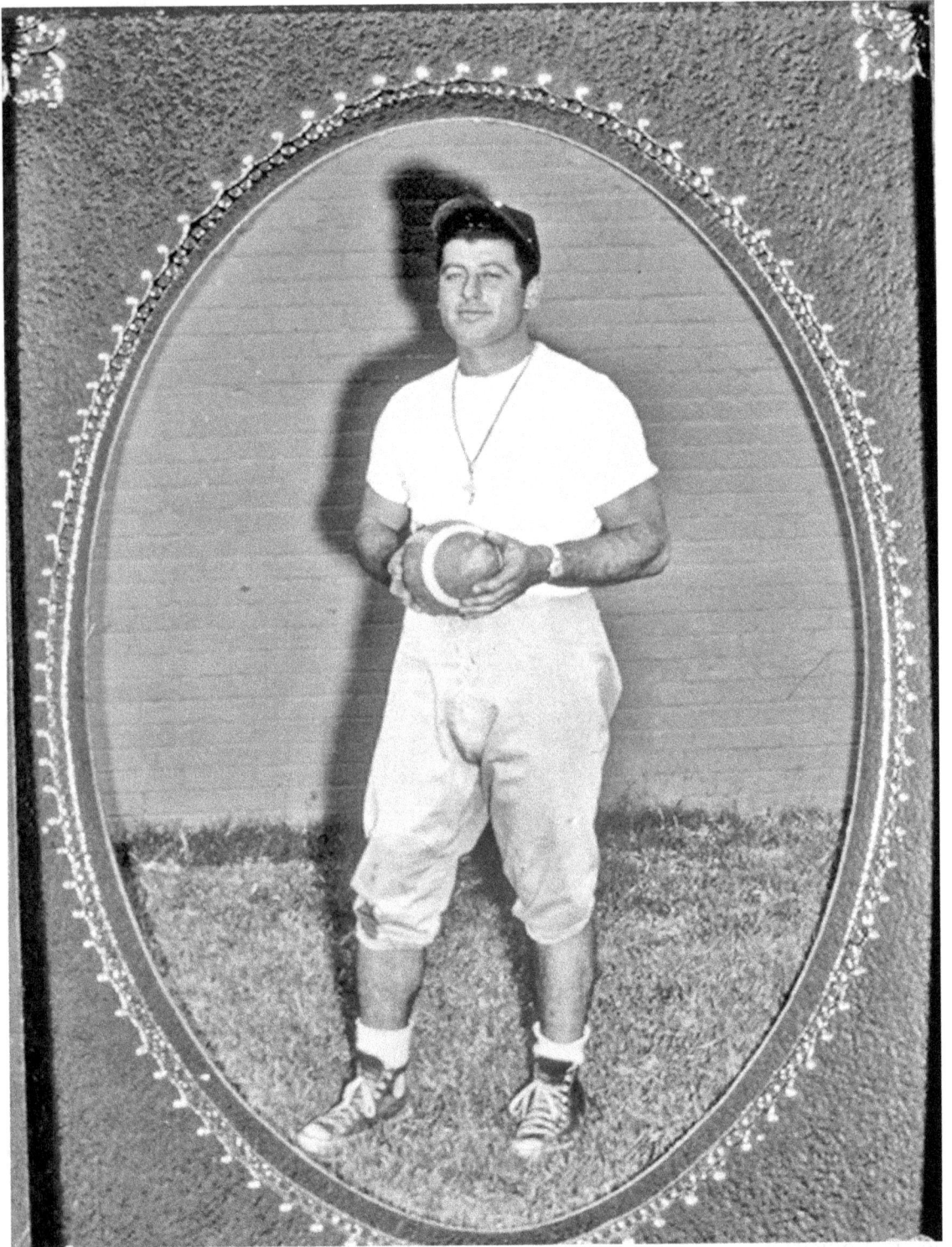

The Famous Case of the Mysterious Bloody Knee

Nephews and nieces—Mitchell Vitkovich, Jeanie Vitkovich, Joan Vitkovich, Jan Bundy, Paul Bundy Shannon, Nicole Michael and Justin Bundy

and Judy Camarinos, Walter Little and
Phillip Little and families.

Cousins—Sid Francies, Phil Francies,
Bob Francies, Teeter Francies, Alex
Nader (Rita) and family, Josie Sawaia of
Scottsdale, Nephew, Karim (Kay and
Dora) Nasser and family of Saskatoon,
Canada along with thousands of friends,
teachers, students athletes and coaches!

Northern Arizona University football coaches with Nasser in the Bulldog Lacker Room in front of the famous picture of Coach Nasser

NAU football coaches with Nasser at the Bulldog "Rock"

**Head Football Coaches: Jerome Souers, Head Coach of NAU Lumberjacks
and Emil Nasser, Former Winslow Coach**

Coach Emil Nasser being toasted by the Winslow Bulldog Cheerleaders

Coach Emil Nasser Presents his Prize Home-grown Zucchini

RECORD OF ACCOMPLISHMENTS
COACHING RECORDS

Football

Winningness Football Coach
Arizona history
243 wins
90 losses
9 ties
3 State Championships
16 Conference Championships
4 Undefeated Seasons

Joseph City High School:
2 State Championships and
2 Conference championships
30 wins and four losses.

Track

3 State Runner-up Champions
10 Conference Championships

Baseball

2 State Runner-up Champions
5 Conference Championships

HALL OF FAME INDUCTIONS

Miami High School Hall of Fame—Charter Member
Northern Arizona University Football Hall of Fame 1971
Arizona Sports Hall of Fame-1971
Arizona Coaches Association Hall of Fame-1984,Charter member
National High School Athletic Coaches Association Hall of Fame—1996-
Arizona Track Coaches Hall Off Fame
Flagstaff Hall of Fame 2013

HONORS

Arizona Coach of the Year—1964
NFL Golden Helmet Award
The Arizona All-Star Coach1949,1965,1979 and
All-Star Game Dedicatee 1982-2003.

APPENDICES

ling comedy, "The Trouble With | Jolson and Ruby Keeler.

Nassar Chooses 49 For First String At Winslow High School

Curtis And Lovett Assist In Handling Players; Game Next Week

Winslow High School football-ers were rounding into shape this week in preparation for the first home game of the season when Snowflake invades the Bulldog gridiron next Saturday, September '20.

Coach Emil Nassar has made a preliminary segregation of his boys into the A Squad and the B Squad, with a large group still reporting for each. The A Squad remains the larger so far, with 49 men in uniform. Of these, the coach says 34 are good prospects for the season's play, although he feels some of the others may show sufficient class to get a berth on the first string in one or more games.

With from three to six men battling for each position, the starting lineup will be in doubt almost up to the hour of the first game, Nassar said. If the coming week develops some outstanding player for each position, the starting lineup against Snowflake may be published next week, but as matters now stand, the coach is undecided on a first team.

Those who have an even chance for the various positions are:

Ends — DeMorse, Castlebury, Fowler, H. Warnock, and Burney.
Tackles—Werner, Walker, G. Warnock, McNeil, Newman, and Miller.
Guards—Archer, Ceballos, Hernandez, Oliver, Millier and Gardner.
Centers — Stevenson, Ames, Bealer, and McNelly.
Quarterbacks—McCormick, Patterson, Jenkins, and Watson.
Fullbacks—Mosley, Stewart and Burgett.
Halfbacks—Ackin, Dominguez, Pisel, Davis, Petronovich and Latin.

Boys whose names do not appear on this list are not ruled out of the possibility of playing, Nassar said. Some late-comers are only now rounding into physical shape, and may do better than their early performances indicate, the coach said.

Scrimmage for the squad began on September 3, and will continue during the remainder of the time before the opening whistle against Snowflake next week. The A squad has been working on pass defense, fundamentals of blocking and tackling, and have done a daily stint of calesthenics. These activities will be continued throughout the season to keep the team in top condition, Nassar said.

Nassar is handling the boys in the backfield on the T—formation and although he says he is far from satisfied, yet there is real progress being made.

James Curtis is at work on the A Squad line and progress there is encouraging. The linemen are responding to the keen competition for positions, and it is expected that the line as well as the backfield will fulfill the coach's desire for speed in all games in which the Bulldogs take the field this season.

James Lovett, B. Squad Coach, is giving his boys thorough training in fundamentals, Nassar said, and will have many of them in line for positions on the first string toward the end of the season, or for future varsity teams.

LODGE MEETING MONDAY

The Ladies Society of the Brotherhood of Locomotive Firemen and Enginemen will meet Monday, September 15, at 2:00 p. m. at the Firemen's Hall. Reports of the recent convention will be given by delegates and all members are urged to attend.

● WATCH FOR OFFICIAL OPENING OF STUDIO GRAND, 217 WEST THIRD. Adv.

BASEBA

Sunday, S

Winslow C

2:30 P

PLAY OFF
NORTHERN ARIZONA

FLAGST

Winslow Opens Season With 12 To 6 Victory Over Snowflake Lobos

By BOB KRYDER

Football got off to a not-so-roaring start in Winslow last Saturday as the Winslow High School Bulldogs defeated the Snowflake Lobos, 12 to 6, in a game ragged from start to finish.

Both teams were on the field under conference competition for the first time this season which probably accounted for "first game rattles." Winslow was slow to take the initiative and both scores came in the last eight minutes of play. Snowflake came to life in the second quarter and scored their lone touchdown.

The first quarter was sparked with several twenty and thirty yard runs only to be called back on penalties or to fall short on ground attacks. From the start of the second quarter, Snowflake became the aggressor and kept the Winslow eleven on their heels constantly. Winslow took the ball on their own 25 yd. line after stopping what appeared to be a Snowflake touchdown march.

The Lobos held Winslow short of a first down and then broke through to partially block the Winslow punt. The Lobos recovered on the Winslow thirty and three plays later Ronald Willis tossed a 15 yard touchdown pass to W. Porter. The point after the touchdown failed and Snowflake led 6 to 0 at the halftime mark.

Fourth Quarter

Late in the fourth quarter Winslow drove the Lobos back to the five yard line where a poor kick put Winslow in scoring position. A long pass ruled as interference set Winslow on the Snowflake five and Mosely carried the ball across for the first Winslow tally.

Winslow kicked off to Snowflake and once more forced the Lobos to punt with their backs rubbing the goal posts. Aiken returned the punt to the 30 and on the next play McCormick tossed to Chich Warnock and put the ball on the one foot line. With two and a quarter minutes remaining, Jack Aiken plunged the winning touchdown. The kick for extra point was blocked.

B

Bulldogs And Eagles Battle To 14 to 14 Draw, Tuesday

Before a huge crowd at Skidmore Field in Flagstaff, and bucking a cold northeast wind, the Winslow Bulldogs and the Flagstaff Eagles battled to a 14 to 14 tie last Tuesday, which also placed the two teams in a deadlock for second place in the Northern Arizona Conference.

The game, marred with penalties, was one of the hardest fought games played this year for both organizations. Winslow took an early lead over Flagstaff in the first quarter and gave evidence of continuing a large score build up. But three holding penalties forced Winslow to lose control of the ball and the Eagles took advantage of the breaks and with a flashy ground attack tied the score at halftime. Neither team scored in the third quarter and Flagstaff broke the ice to score with five minutes gone in the fourth quarter. Later in the fourth, with approximately a minute remaining in the game, Winslow scored the tying tally.

Both teams played well on the defensive with Burgett. Mosely, Watson, Akin and Dominguez sparking the Bulldogs' offensive and Evans Jakle and Garcia heading Flagstaff's attack.

First Quarter

Burgett booted the opening kickoff deep into Eagle territory and Garcia returned the ball to the 20 yard line. The Eagles rolled off two first downs bringing the ball to the 47. On the next play McCormick intercepted an Eagle pass and Winslow took over on the Flagstaff 36. Dominguez hit the line on the first two plays and rolled off 8 yards. The third play failed to gain with an incompleted pass and on the fourth down Burgett went for four yards giving Winslow a first down on the

(Continued On Page Two)

C

Bulldogs And . . . .

(Continued From Page One)
Eagle 26 yard line. The first play was an incompleted pass and on the second play, Dominguez went for four yards. On the third play Burgett scampered around the right end and went the remaining distance for the first score of the game. Akin plunged for the extra point and the Bulldogs were in front 7 to 0 at the quarter's end.

Second Quarter

After an exchange of fumbles midway in the second quarter, Flagstaff took over on their own 41 yard line. The Winslow defense tightened and two Eagle passes were knocked down. Jakle took the ball on a quick opening play through the right side of the line and ran 60 yards for the first Eagle tally. Evans plunged the point and the half ended with board showing a 7 to 7 tie.

Fourth Quarter

Flagstaff took over on their own 25 midway through the fourth quarter and Garcia, Jakle and Evans alternately lugged the ball to the Winslow 29. Jakle ripped off a first down to the 15. Garcia picked up three yards on the first play and on the second play carried for two. On the third play Evans was nailed for a yard loss and on the fourth, Garcia passed to Soto on the goal line who fell over for the touchdown. The plunge for extra point clicked and Flagstaff edged ahead 14 to 7.

Flagstaff booted and Winslow took over on the 35. Akin rolled off 7 yards, Watson one, and on the third play was stopped for no gain. Then Danny Watson cocked his arm and in three passes, each one going to Dominguez, moved the ball to the Flagstaff 18. Burgett took the ball, faked a pass, and skirted the right side for the touchdown. Mosely bulled his way into the end zone for the extra point and the game ended seconds later.

D

Bill Burgett Skirts Left End for a Nice Gain Against the Flagstaff Eagles

A number of Winslow football players gained All-Northern Arizona and All-State recognition this year. Among them were the following:

Northern First Team:	Bruce DeMarse _____ End Gene Hernandez _____ Guard Jim McNelly _____ Center
Northern Second Team:	Dan Watson ___ Quarterback Boyd Lee _____ Tackle Louis Lee _____ Halfback
Northern Honorable Mention:	Bill Burgett _____ Fullback Bill Gardner _____ Tackle
All State Second Team:	Dan Watson _____ Back
All State Third Team:	Bruce DeMarse _____ End
All State Honorable Mention:	Louis Lee _____ Back Joe Hernandez _____ Guard

Back Row: Coach Nasser, Paul Lattin, Dan Watson, Bill Burgett, Louis Lee.
Front Row: George Warnock, Bill Gardner, Gene Hernandez, Jim McNelly, Bill Ames, Buddy Campbell, Bruce DeMarse.

F—First Victory Over Prescott In 37 Years — 1948

Winslow Rolls Over Prescott First Time Since 1937 Game

Winslow Mail

2 ★   Winslow, Arizona
Friday, October 29, 1948

(Bulldog Barks)

Winslow's Bulldogs overpowered the Prescott Badgers to the tune of a 26-7 score last Friday night at Prescott. This victory definitely establishes Winslow as a contender for the state "B" class football championship. Superior, Douglas and Winslow are the only three undefeated teams in state class "B" play.

Winslow received the kickoff and ran it back to their own 45 yard line. Then the Bulldogs opened up with a terrific ground offensive which covered yards in nine plays and ended when Louis Lee toted the ball to paydirt. Watson passed to Burgett for the extra point.

In the second period, Lattin plunged over from the six yard line and Watson passed to Warnock for the conversion. Winslow 14; Prescott 0. In the dying minutes of the first half, Badger quarterback, Bill Melvin, passed to Joe Perez from his own 30 yard line in a play which netted 70 yards and six points. The kick was good. Halftime — Winslow 14; Prescott 7.

Immediately after the third period opened, Watson slung a twenty yard pass from his own 35, and Burgett put on a display of speed and amazing brokenfield running to sprint 45 yards to a touchdown.

Watson passed to Warnock early in the fourth quarter for another counter to put the Bulldogs in the lead 26-7. The remainder of the period was spent by the Bulldogs in Prescott territory as they tried to widen the margin of victory. Co-captains for the game were Burgett and Watson.

This was the first Winslow victory over Prescott since 1937, when the Bulldogs downed the Badger 7-0. According to his unique and daring system, Coach Nasser played the entire squad in at least one period, thus giving all the boys on the squad an opportunity to learn the fundamentals of the game in the best possible way—by experience.

The linup with starter's name first:

Ends: Jennings, Warnock, Noel and Eastman.

Tackles: Campbell, Werner, Gardner, Boyd Lee.

Guards: Ames, Hernandez, Dickson, Miller, Howell.

Centers: McNelly, Keller, Feagins.

Quarterbacks: Watson, McCormick, Cooata.

Halfbacks: Lattin, Louis Lee, Jenkins, Pisel.

Fullbacks: Burgett, Petronavich, Clark.

WINSLOW YOUTH IS LIGHTWEIGHT CHAMP OF TEXAS

"Chief" Gordon House, Winslow Indian, has just won the Texas State Lightweight boxing championship at Galveston, according to information received here this week.

His championship bout was fought October 20, and is described as one of the most sensational ever to be presented at Galveston.

House is now champion of three states in his weight class,

F

G—Honored Bulldogs Of The 1950 Team

Honored   *Bulldogs*

Buddy "Gordo" Campbell was the first Winslow Bulldog in many years to be selected on the first team All-State. He won the selection while playing fullback, but received a half-back position on the honorable team. Besides this outstanding honor, Buddy was also selected as one of the outstanding players in the Northern Conference.

Co-captain Campbell played first string on three varsity Bulldog squads, one of which was State Co-champion.

John Paul, Bulldog quarter-back, was selected as quarterback on the second string All-State team. He was also chosen as one of the thirty-three outstanding players in the Northern Conference.

Frank Santistevan, vicious guard on the Bulldog squad, was selected as one of the thirty-three outstanding players in the Northern conference and also co-captain of the squad.

Bill Church, center of the Bulldog line, is co-captain of the squad; he was selected as an outstanding player in the Northern conference and also received honorable mention on the All-State team.

1955 CLASS "A" NORTH CHAMPS

"A" SQUAD

FIRST ROW: Duane Robinson, Manuel Vargas, Barry Mack, Winstel Belton, Delano Blanks, Jim Fergus, Joe McAdams, Terry Lacy, Bob Gray, Lee Wasdon, Lee Curnutte, Arden McRae, Roger Coffey, Charles Bumgarner, Don Williams, Bill Armstrong, Mike Cooper, Charles Rose, Reyes Rodriquez, Bob Belton, John Dunigan, Emil Nasser, Ron McCarthy, Mel Hannah, Justo Lomeli, Kent Randall, Don Hodge, Paul Reynolds, Joe Gallegos, Tom Crimmins, Gene Goldsberry, Dave Vanderkraats, and James Curtis.

Your words echo into eternity
You did it all for us—we will never forget you

I—1955 Champs Scenes and Players

THE RUGGED ELEVEN—RIGHT TO LEFT—Ron McCarthy, Gene Goldsberry, Joe Gallegos, Charles Rose, Tom Crimmings, Paul Reynolds, Arden McRae, Coach Curtis, Lee Wasdon, Bob Gray, Terry Lacy, Bob Belton, Coach Nasser.

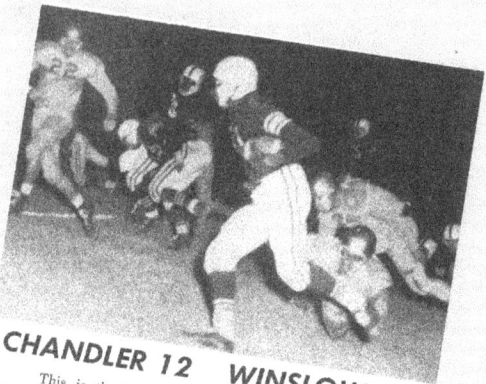

CHANDLER 12 WINSLOW 14

This is the kind of game you always remember!

CONFERENCE SCHEDULE

Winslow	48	0	Flagstaff
Winslow	14	12	Chandler
Winslow	13	0	Tempe
Winslow	14	7	Prescott
Winslow	40	13	Sunnyslope
Winslow	36	7	Tolleson

SEASON RECORD

Won 7
Lost 3

GENE GOLDSBERRY	LEE WASDON	JOE GALLEGOS	RON McCARTHY
Tackle	Halfback	Tackle	Guard
All-Conference	*All-Conference*	*All-Conference*	*All-Conference*
All-State	*All-State*	*All-State*	*Homecoming*
Captain	*Captain*	*Honorable Mention*	*King*
Honorable Mention			
All-American			

109

J—1955 Champs Scenes and Players

Coach Nasser and Coach Curtis backed up by fifteen Seniors.

MANUEL VARGAS
Quarterback

PAUL REYNOLDS
Tackle
All-Conference
Honorable Mention

BOB BELTON
Halfback
All-Conference
Honorable Mention

BILL ARMSTRONG
End

WINSLOW 48   FLAG 0
Lee scores his first TD of the season.

BOB GRAY
Fullback
All-Conference
Honorable Mention

MEL HANNAH
End

DON WILLIAMS
End

JOE McADAMS
Halfback

J

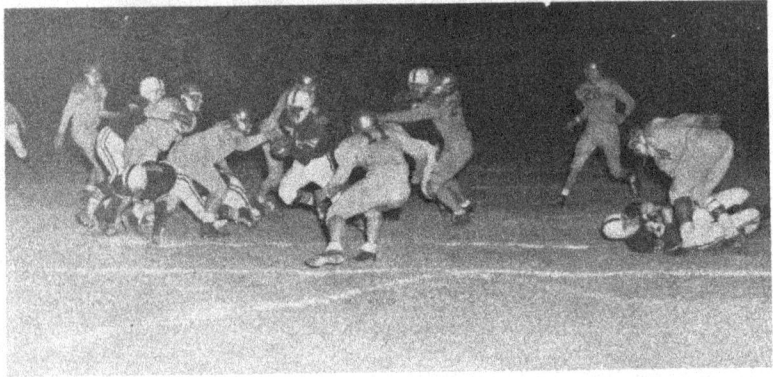

WINSLOW 14   PRESCOTT 7

The break through after a long drive.

BARRY MACK
Quarterback

SUNNYSLOPE 13   WINSLOW 40

Gray has a whole team after him.

DON HODGE
Guard

Mr. Freeman is getting a sample of Granddaddy.

BOBBY ROBINSON
Guard

CHARLES BUMGARNER
Tackle

K

TEMPE 0 WINSLOW 13

Tempe didn't have a chance.

JIM FERGUS
Guard

ARDEN McRAE
End

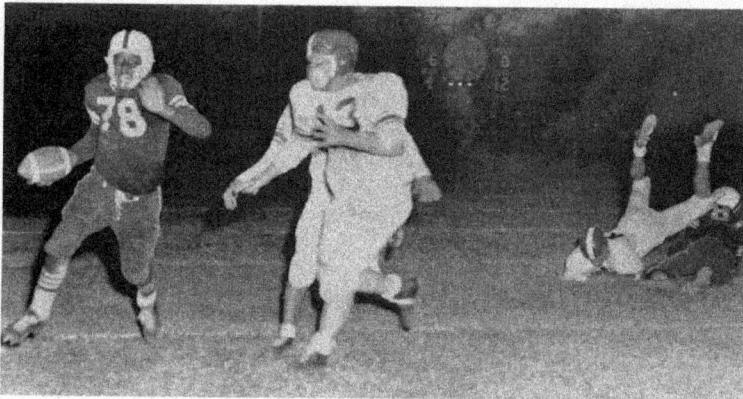

TOLLESON 7 WINSLOW 36

Wasdon turns it on around left end for another TD.

TERRY LACY Quarterback	ROGER COFFEY End	CHARLES ROSE Center	TOM CRIMMINS Guard	REYES RODRIQUEZ Center

N— Nasser Wall of Hall of Fame at 210 Mahoney, Winslow

O— 1964 Championship Team Official Picture

4th Row: Coach Nasser, Earl Owens, Bill Baca, Mike Madeo, Art Griffith, Arthur, Coach Weatherton. 3rd Row: Jim Caldwell, Ricky Donnelly, Lloyd Garner, Curtis Bardsley, Steve MacArthur, Pat Beckwith. 2nd Row: John O'Haco, Jerry Easley, Bill Heath, Bill Bolin. 1st Row: Rusty Meikle, Wal- Jim Store.

Charles Mayberry, Robert Short, Mike Lopez, Garry Winans, Trainer Mac-Taylor, Willie Fish, Warren Hardy, George Welsh, Mike Peart, Steve Martinez, David Riley, Fred Basgal, Mike Sullivan, Bill Luther, Mike ter Van, Tom Kamuho, Tine Lopez, Keith Rhodes, Bill Cherry, John Hysong

Varsity Football Scoreboard

Winslow 33	0	Holbrook
Winslow 13	6	Prescott
Winslow 32	7	Dysart
Winslow 39	6	Snowflake
Winslow 26	14	Paradise Valley
Winslow 13	6	Peoria
Winslow 52	0	Phoenix Indian
Winslow 14	0	Tolleson
Winslow 34	7	Phoenix Christian

State Championship Game

Winslow 7	0	Flowing Wells

256 pts by Bulldogs   Opponents = 36 pts   TOTAL POINTS

O

P— 1964 Championship Team Scenes and Players

OFFENSIVE BACKFIELD

Mike Sullivan, Mike Madeo, Mike O'Haco, Tine Lopez

Class 'A'
Honorable Mention

ALL STATE

Steve Garner
Art Griffith
Garry Winans
Pat Beckwith
Mike O'Haco

Looks like Tine is in a tight spot.

Members of the 1st
Team of Class 'A'

ALL STATE
Mike Lopez
Mike Peart
Tine Lopez
Mike Madeo

Q— 1964 Championship Team Scenes and Players

DEFENSIVE LINE

Mike Peart, Bill Heath, Mike Lopez, Gary Winens, Robert Short, Bill Bolin, Bill Luther

Mike O'Haco dodging a Prescott Badger.

CLASS "A" NORTH

2ND TEAM

Art Griffith
Pat Beckwith
Mike Sullivan

CLASS "A"

John Hysong in a spectacular play
against Prescott.

R— 1964 Championship Team Scenes and Players

DEFENSIVE BACKS

Mike Sullivan, Mike Madeo, John Hysong, Rusty Miekle

ALL CONFERENCE

HONORABLE MENTION

Mike O'Haco
Mike Lopez
Garry Winens

CHAMPIONS

Earl Owens (82), Mike O'Haco (68), Bill Baca (83), and Mike Sullivan (65) provide a hole for Tine Lopez (55) against Peoria.

Tine Lopez showing off some fancy footwork.

Bulldogs Playing For State Title Tonight

Winslow's Bulldogs are facing Flowing Wells on the Caballeros' home field in Tucson tonight for the state Class A championship.

Game time is 8 p.m.

Radio KINO will carry a play by play description of the game as it happens, and the Daily Mail will round up the game and the season Monday night in permanent printed form.

Busloads of Winslow residents left this morning as rooters set out to watch the Bulldogs, and the team itself left early for the game.

The Bulldogs are undefeated so far this year.

Top players of the season will be honored Monday night at the annual Quarterback Club Football Banquet at the Elks Lodge auditorium.

U Of A-ASU Game Splits Prophets

By Bob Eger
AP Sports Writer

Pessimism flowed freely from the rival camps this week as Arizona State University and the University of Arizona prepared for their annual football battle Saturday night in

S

WINSLOW Daily Mail

| Volume Eighty-Four | Winslow, Arizona, Monday, November 30, 1964 | (Associated Press Leased Wire) | Number 94 |

Bulldogs Win Third State Crown

Football Squad Closes An Undefeated Season

Winslow high school's undefeated Bulldogs won the third state sports championship in 1964 last Friday evening by defeating Flowing Wells 7-0 on the Caballeros' home field for the football crown.

Players and coaching staff will be honored tonight at the annual Quarterback Club banquet at 6:30 in the Elks auditorium.

The Bulldogs' football title follows state baseball and wrestling championships last spring, third in the state in track, and conference champs in basketball, all within the last year.

The Bulldog defensive unit held another opponent scoreless as the team ran up its tenth victory for the season.

Timing Hurt

The long layoff between the Bulldogs' final game and the championship battle showed in weak timing through most of the first half of Friday's game, but the team finally

shook the doldrums just before halftime, driving from the Winslow 30 to the Flowing Wells 26. Penalties and a dropped pass prevented a touchdown as the clock ran out.

The Bulldogs held Flowing Wells to nine yards from scrimmage in the third quarter.

Winning Score

In the final quarter, the two teams exchanged punts. Finally the Caballeros ran a punt return to the Winslow 29 yard line, and in seven plays were on the Winslow 3 yard line with a first down.

Ed Weaver was stopped for a one yard loss on the first

(Continued on Page 8)

THE TOUCHDOWN — Quarterback Tino Lopez, on the bottom of this stack (arrow) holds the football and the touchdown which completed the Bulldogs' undefeated season and made the team state Class A champions last Friday night. Standing is Caballero fullback Larry White; identifiable on the ground are 'Dog guard David Riley and tackle Mike Lopez. (Bergman Photo)

Rail Strike
Talks Reopen

MORE ABOUT —
Football Squad

(Continued From Page 1)
play; then got to the one yard line on a second play before the entire left side of the Bulldog line nailed him and the ball squirted from his grasp.

Bill Bollin pounced on the ball for a touchback, and the 'Dogs had possession of the ball on their own 20 yard line.

Nine Plays

In nine plays the Bulldogs reeled off 80 yards to a touchdown.

Mike O'Haco was the first carrier, picking up five yards in two tries. A 32 yard Lopez to Jerry Easley pass was called back, but Mike Madeo blasted his way up the middle for 14 yards and the first down.

Mike Sullivan got in the act next, with a ground carry, followed by a Lopez to Mike Peart pass; then O'Haco got through the line, reversed his field, and aided by some fine downfield blocking, made it to the Flowing Wells 11 yard line. Madeo picked up seven yards and O'Haco three more to put the 'Dogs on the Caballeros' one yard line.

Quarterback Tine Lopez handled the ball carrying chores himself on the next play, a quarterback sneak, and scored the TD, following up by calmly kicking the PAT. The clock showed one minute 35 seconds left.

Final Try

Flowing Wells made a last try at scoring, and an over-eager Bulldog defense took two penalties, but held the Caballeros even when they took to the air.

In a post game effort to pick the outstanding players, head coach Emil Nasser named practically the entire varsity roster. Twenty eight players saw action, and players not on the field stood or knelt at the sidelines and shouted encouragement to their teammates.

Praised

The defensive unit's Garry Winans, Mike Lopez, Robert Short, Bill Bollin, Bill Heath, Mike Peart, Mike Madeo, Jerry Easley, John Martinez, Rusty Meikle, Mike Sullivan, and John Hysong drew special praise.

On offense, quarterback Tine Lopez, and backs Mike O'Haco, Mike Sullivan, Mike Madeo, and Jerry Easley drew praise.

Given special mention were linemen Pat Beckwith, Steve McArthur, Fred Basgal, Earl Owens, Artie Griffith, Mike Lopez, George Welsh, Steve Garner, and Mike Peart.

Nasser singled out the kick-off team for note, along with Lloyd Taylor's kicking and Rick Donnelly's punting.

Associate coach Carl Weatherton, who was called out of town on an emergency just before the game, received thanks.

Herman McArthur, team trainer, took care of minor injuries all season, Nasser said, and the team had remarkably few injuries at all, he added.

Managers Jim Caldwell, Tony Cullum, and Danny Nasser were also praised.

MORE ABOUT —
No Compromise

(Continued from Page 1)
matters until after the first of the year so that there would be no occasion to question the voting rights of the Soviet Union.

Under Article 19 the Soviets stand to lose their vote in the General Assembly because they have fallen more than two years behind in their dues.

U

Page Four · WINSLOW DAILY MAIL · Monday, November 30, 1964

ESCAPE TRY—Mike Sullivan (65) tries to evade the Caballeros' John Cirelli (21) during last Friday night's state championship game on Flowing Wells' home field. (Bergman Photo)

WELCOME HOME — Bulldogs were greeted by a 38 car parade and a crowd of hundreds as the state Class A champions returned to Winslow by bus after their defeat of Flowing Wells last Friday. (Bergman Photo)

LOPEZ CARRYING — An unidentified Caballero stops Winslow's Tine Lopez as the Bulldog quarterback tries to make it to the goal line. Guard Earl Owens (82) is on his way to stop another tackler. (Bergman Photo)

RELAX — Bulldogs went for a swim, in uniforms, immediately after winning the state championship, with Coach Emil Nasser leading the way. Shown are Walter Van and Bill Bollin. (Bergman Photo)

Bulldogs Dominate All Conference Selections

Winslow Bulldogs, state Class A football Champions, dominated the selections for Class A North All Star teams, announced this week. The Bulldogs placed three men on the All Conference First Team, three more on the All Conference Second Team, and three additional ones received Honorable Mention.

First Team members from Winslow were fullback Mike Madeo, quarterback Florentino "Tine" Lopez, and left end, Mike Peairl.

Second Team choices from Winslow were right tackle Artie Griffith, center Pat Beckwith and left halfback Mike Sullivan.

Honorable Mention from Winslow were halfback Mike O'Haco, and linemen Mike Lopez and Garry Winans.

Other Navajo County schools represented were Snowflake with Bob Hall of Snowflake at right guard on the first team, Cary Cosper at fullback on the second team, and Ron Foil, Charles Hendrickson and Fred Hunt in honorable mention. Also Holbrook with Oliver Strong, Grant Benson and Elmer Sangster among the honorable mention.

Tolleson trailed Winslow in the all-conference honors with two on the first team, two on the second team, and four among honorable mention.

Kingman was third on the conference with two on the first team, two on the second team, and three in honorable mention.

Beavers Won In Irish Vs. Trojans

By Bob Green
AP Sports Writer

The only winner in the Southern California - Notre Dame game was the Oregon State Beavers, and they weren't even there.

The jubilant Beavers were picked over Southern California and named the West Coast representative in the Rose Bowl Saturday, just a few hours after the Trojans had turned in the upset of the year in a brilliant, 10-17 come-from-behind triumph over Notre Dame, the nation's top-ranked college football team.

Southern Cal's Craig Fertig was the chief factor in the amazing upset of the Irish, who had won nine straight under new coach Ara Parseghina.

Trailing 17-0 at half, the Trojans got one touchdown in the third period, cut it to 17-13 on a 22-yard Fertig touchdown pass and won it in the fourth quarter with less than two minutes to go on another Fertig touchdown toss.

Georgia stopped Georgia Tech 7-0 and immediately accepted the Sun Bowl bid in another major game on the last full weekend of the college football season.

Army, meanwhile, finally broke the five-year Navy jinx and edged the Middies 11-8 on Barry Nickerson's 20-yard, fourth-quarter field goal.

The Rev. and Mrs. Powell Green and John had Larry Bergman, Harold Ryerson and Mrs. Leo Graff and Marsha and Larry as dinner guests for Thanksgiving.

V

Tuesday, December 1, 1964   WINSLOW DAILY MAIL   Page Three

Championship Team Honored At Annual Quarterback Club Banquet

"If a player gives everything he has—100 per cent—that is all anyone can ask of him," said head coach Frank Kush of the Arizona State University Sun Devils in addressing the Winslow Football Banquet last evening at the Elks Auditorium.

Coach Kush was featured speaker at the annual gathering where Florentino "Tine" Lopez and Mike Madeo were chosen co-captains of the 1964 Bulldog State Football Champions, and where coaches, players and boosters were recognized as the season closed.

More than 400 parents, players, coaches, school personnel and students crowded the auditorium to hail the champions and the other football players of Winslow High School.

Thirty-four varsity players and two varsity managers were honored as the climax to the evening's plaudits. Certificates had already been awarded to 40 junior varsity players and two managers, and to 51 freshmen players and three managers.

In expressing appreciation for the work of the football staff at all three levels, High School Principal J. L. Curtis said 165 boys had turned out this season for football and 134 of them had stayed to the end of the season.

Coach Kush told the boys, and the rest incidentally, that winning is not enough, and is not all important. "Wanting to win is everything," he said, if the individual does his best. This is just as important in the classroom and in other activities of life as it is on the football field, he stressed.

There are some guiding principles which are important on the football field, and in life, coach Kush said:

"Don't curse!
"Don't gripe!
"Don't alibi!
"Don't get discouraged!"

Dr. Harry Simmons was master of ceremonies for the annual Quarterback Banquet, jointly sponsored by the Elks and Babbitts.

After the invocation by Fr. Richard Milligan, James Nottingham, Loyal Knight, welcomed the football players and their supporters. Appreciation was expressed by Curtis, after which Dr. Simmons introduced guests, including sponsors, coaches, and committee members.

Head Coach Emil Nasser reviewed the season, then introduced Ellis McIntosh who presented certificates to the freshman team, assisted by Dean Stotts.

Nasser then introduced coach Jim Freeman who presented the junior varsity with certificates, assisted by Alvin Fritz.

Lobos Can't Get Ahead By Winning

By Bob Eger
AP Sports Writer

New Mexico's Lobos have discovered that the better they get, the tougher it is to run away from the rest of the league in the Western Athletic Conference football title chase.

The Lobos concluded their best season in history Saturday with a 9-7 victory over Kansas State.

Just a few hours later, Arizona trounced arch-rival Arizona State University 30-6 to finish in a three-way tie with the Lobos and Utah for conference championship.

The varsity squad then was introduced and received their letters. Nottingham presented Elks awards to Everett Patterson, art teacher, coach Carl Weatherton in absentia, and to coach Nasser.

W. M. Wright, assistant high school principal, introduced the guest speaker.

Following the address, the Pep Squad lead in the singing of the WHS Alma Mater.

Other awards, from the teams, went to Trainer Herman McArthur and coaches Weatherton and Nasser.

Varsity lettermen named were these:

Bill Baca, Curtis Bardsley, Fred Basgal, Pat Beckwith, Bill Bollin, Bill Cherry, Ricky Donnelly, Jerry Easley, Willie Fish, Steve Garner, Art Griffith, Warren Hardy, Bill Heath, John Hysong, Tom Kanuho, Mike Lopez, Tine Lopez, Mike Madeo, John Martinez, Charles Mayberry, Steve McArthur, Rusty Meikle, Mike O'Haco, Earl Owens, Mike Peart, Keith Rhodes, David Riley, Robert Short, Jim Storr, Mike Sullivan, Lloyd Taylor, Walter Van, George Welsh, Garry Winans, Jim Caldwell, Mgr., Spec. cert. Danny Nasser, Mgr., John Madeo (honorary).

Mr. and Mrs. Wayne L. Troutner and Mr. and Mrs. J. Morris Richards attended evening services at the LDS Church in Woodruff Sunday evening. The men were speakers at the services.

CAPTAINS — Tine Lopez, left, and Mike Madeo, right, were named co-captains of the 1964 Bulldog state football champs. They are shown with Frank Kush, ASU Coach and featured speaker at the Quarterback Banquet. (Bergman Photo)

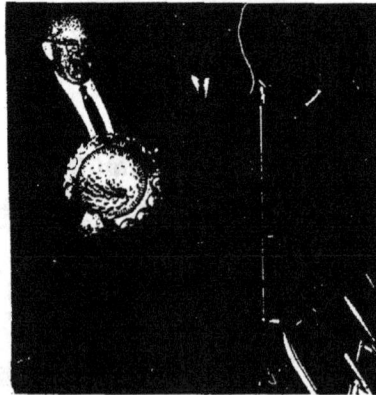

HERO OF THE YEAR — Trainer Herman McArthur was awarded this gold tray by the Bulldog varsity football team Monday night in appreciation of his efforts for the team as the players named him their "hero" of the year. His son Steve, a varsity player, background, made the presentation. (Bergman Photo)

X —   Nasser and Benham in the Emil Nasser Football Foundation Mobile

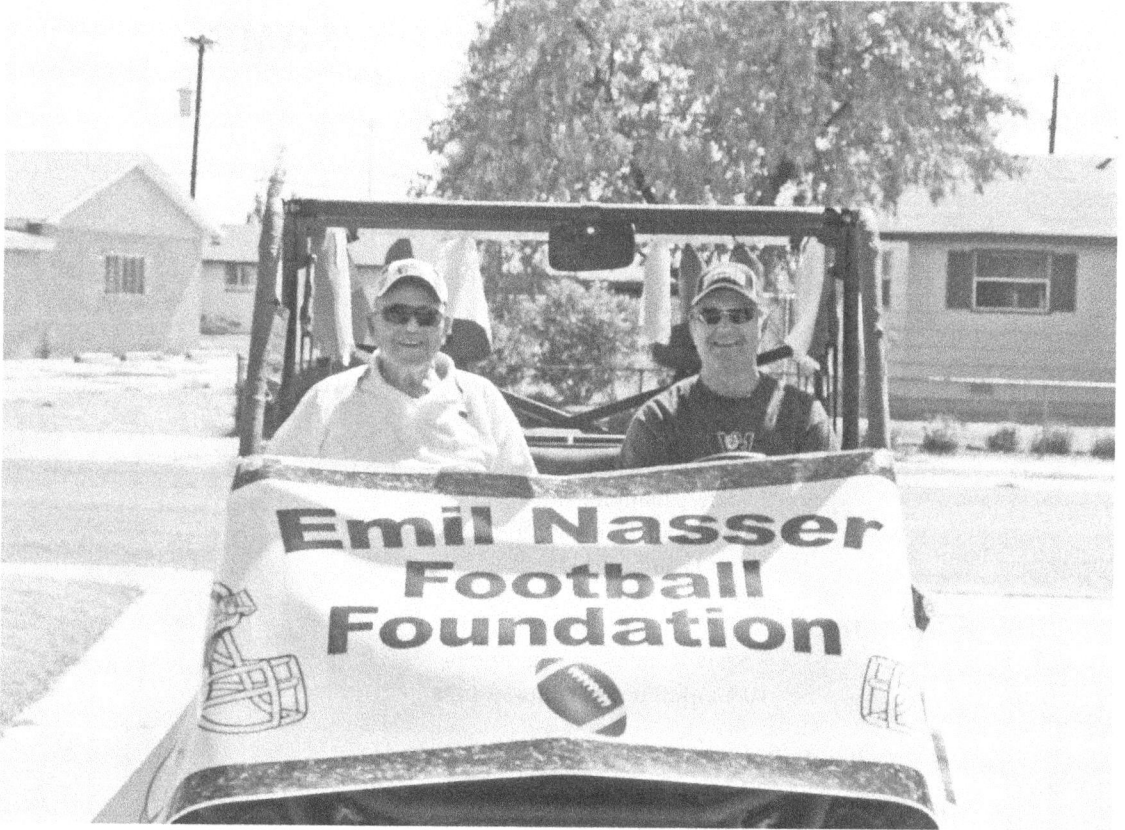

RECORD OF ACCOMPLISHMENT
COACHING RECORDS

FOOTBALL

Winningness Football Coach
Arizona history
243 wins
90 losses
9 ties
3 State Championships
16 Conference Championships
4 Undefeated Seasons

Joseph City High School:
2 State Championships and
2 Conference championships
30 wins and four losses.

Track

3 State Runner-up Champions
10 Conference Championships

Baseball

2 State Runner-up Champions
5 Conference Championships

HALL OF FAME INDUCTIONS

Miami High School Hall of Fame
Northern Arizona University Football Hall of Fame 1971
Arizona Sports Hall of Fame-1971
Arizona Coaches Association Hall of Fame-1984,Charter member
National High School Athletic Coaches Association Hall of Fame-

1996

Flagstaff Hall of Fame 2013

HONORS

Arizona Coach of the Year—1964
NFL Golden Helmet Award
The Arizona All-Star Coach1949,1965,1979 and
All-Star Game Dedicatee 1982-2003.

"Coach, you gave me a chance and it changed my life for-ever."

Freshman, Right End
Varsity Starter
Jerry, "Rusty," Knowles
Flagstaff, Arizona
November 12, 1947

Z

Forever